F. Scott Fitzgerald

A SHORT AUTOBIOGRAPHY

Edited by James L. W. West III

SCRIBNER

New York   London   Toronto   Sydney

SCRIBNER
A Division of Simon & Schuster, Inc.
1230 Avenue of the Americas
New York, NY 10020

First Scribner trade paperback edition August 2011

SCRIBNER and design are registered trademarks of The Gale Group, Inc.,
used under license by Simon & Schuster, Inc., the publisher of this work.

For information about special discounts for bulk purchases,
please contact Simon & Schuster Special Sales
at 1-866-506-1949 or business@simonandschuster.com.

The Simon & Schuster Speakers Bureau can bring authors to your live event.
For more information or to book an event, contact the Simon & Schuster
Speakers Bureau at 1-866-248-3049 or visit our website
at www.simonspeakers.com.

DESIGNED BY ERICH HOBBING

Manufactured in the United States of America

5   7   9   10   8   6   4

Library of Congress Cataloging-in-Publication Data is available.

ISBN 978-1-4391-9906-0
ISBN 978-1-4391-9907-7 (ebook)

Contents

Preface

"I have cleaner hands in the case of non-fiction
than in fiction."
—Fitzgerald to Maxwell Perkins,
April 2, 1936

This book presents a selection of F. Scott Fitzgerald's
personal writings from 1920 to 1940, the entire span of
his professional career. He was a fine autobiographical
writer, blessed with a supple style, a capacious memory,
and a great fund of experience on which to draw. He
wrote about himself with insight and humor, adopting
poses and reinventing himself as the occasion required.
In his earliest efforts he was exuberant and cocky, though
unsure about how to manage his new fame; during his
middle years he was serious and professional-minded,
addressing problems of authorship and inspiration; in the
late pieces he was reflective and elegiac, looking back on
the Jazz Age, which he had named, with affection and
only a few regrets.

Twice during the last decade of his life, once in 1934
and again in 1936, Fitzgerald proposed a collection such
as this one to Maxwell Perkins, his editor at Charles
Scribner's Sons. "I have never published any personal
stuff between covers because I have needed it all for my
fiction," Fitzgerald wrote to Perkins on May 15, 1934.

"Nevertheless, a good many of my articles and random pieces have attracted a really quite wide attention." Perkins was skeptical about such a book and suggested that a volume of stories might sell more briskly. Fitzgerald obliged by assembling one of his best collections of short fiction, *Taps at Reveille*, which Scribner's published in the spring of 1935, and which performed moderately well at the bookshops, selling some 5,000 copies.

Fitzgerald did not, however, abandon the idea of putting together a collection of his personal writings. He again proposed such a book to Perkins in the spring of 1936, about a year after *Taps at Reveille* was published. "The greater part of these articles are intensely personal," he explained; "that is to say, while a newspaper man has to find something to write his daily or weekly article about, I have written articles entirely when the impetus came from within." Perkins remained lukewarm: "You write non-fiction wonderfully well," he said. "Your observations are brilliant and acute, and your presentations of real characters . . . most admirable." But Perkins had doubts about the appeal of such a collection to readers and suggested that Fitzgerald write a different kind of book, "a reminiscent book,—not autobiographical, but reminiscent." Fitzgerald must have been intrigued by Perkins' suggestion, but in the spring of 1936 he needed to invest his creative energies in producing stories for the high-paying magazines and, he hoped, in writing a new novel. He could not justify composing, from the ground up, the kind of book Perkins had in mind. Fitzgerald put the idea for a collection of personal writings on hold and did not mention it again in his letters to Perkins. In the summer of 1937 he departed from North Carolina, where he had been living, and traveled to the West Coast to take a scriptwriting job with Metro-Goldwyn-Mayer. He spent his last years in Hollywood and died there in

December 1940, with a new novel called *The Last Tycoon* under way, but without having brought his autobiographical writings together into a book.

If Fitzgerald had been able to publish such a collection, it would have given him a chance to reclaim control of his public image. He had not worried much about that image during the early years of his career. He had always been depicted in the press as a handsome, talented, successful young author. He and his wife, Zelda, had become celebrities: they had learned how to charm interviewers and how to provide dependably good copy. During the 1930s, however, Fitzgerald's relationship with the press deteriorated, reaching a low point on September 25, 1936, when a reporter named Michel Mok published an exposé of him in the *New York Post*. This piece, entitled "The Other Side of Paradise," presented Fitzgerald as a washed-up alcoholic, mired in self-pity. A collection of personal writings would have given Fitzgerald a chance to counter this image and present himself in a different light—as a mature and thoughtful literary artist.

In 1945, five years after Fitzgerald's death, his friend Edmund Wilson assembled a collection of the nonfiction and published it with New Directions under the title *The Crack-Up*. This volume was made up of late pieces, all composed during the final seven years of Fitzgerald's life. To these writings Wilson added some selections from the notebooks, two collaborations with Zelda, and several letters from contemporaries praising Fitzgerald's work. *The Crack-Up* presents Fitzgerald as an apologist for the 1920s, a chronicler of remorse and regret, and a student of failure and lost hope. There is nothing incorrect about this image, but it has come, perhaps unduly, to dominate writing and thinking about him. This is not the image that he wanted to present when he made his proposals to Perkins in 1934 and 1936.

The items in the present volume show another side of Fitzgerald—extroverted, witty, and very much in tune with his times. Many of these pieces emphasize his playfulness and sense of fun. They also show his seriousness about the craft of writing and his acute interest in his contemporaries. Highlights include "Who's Who—and Why," "What I Think and Feel at 25," and an amusing self-interrogation called "An Interview with Mr. Fitzgerald," all written early in his career to satisfy the curiosity of his public. "Princeton," which draws on his years as a college student, is filled with mixed emotions: regret for his failures as an undergraduate mingled with admiration for what his university had come to represent. "How to Live on $36,000 a Year" and "How to Live on Practically Nothing a Year" are very funny essays about how money slips through the fingers of the newly prosperous. The mysteries of literary inspiration are explored in "One Hundred False Starts" and "Afternoon of an Author," both addressed to anyone who aspires to make a living by putting words to paper. "The Death of My Father" is a meditation on the senior Fitzgerald, a man who represented for his son an earlier period of gentility and good manners. "A Short Autobiography" (a catalogue of potations imbibed) and "Salesmanship in the Champs-Élysées" (a take on the French and their droll ways) are amusing bagatelles. "My Generation," written near the end of Fitzgerald's life, is a look back at the times through which he had lived and the people who had shaped his era.

It's worth mentioning that Fitzgerald wrote the items in this collection for money. He was a professional author with no other job, no trust fund, and no independent source of income. He made his way on what he earned with his pen. He kept a record of funds received in a personal ledger: for the pieces published in this collection he was paid a total of $9,225. This sum translates into more than $100,000 in buying power today. Fitzgerald published these pieces in prominent outlets, including the *New Yorker*, *The Bookman*, the *Saturday Evening Post*, *College Humor*, *American Magazine*, *Ladies' Home Journal*, and *Esquire*. He knew how to reach his audience; he also knew how to be compensated for what he wrote. He wanted to make money *and* to be taken seriously—a difficult combination for any author to pull off. The pieces collected here are amusing to read but are also full of keen insights about American society, ambition and fame, the expatriate scene in Europe, and the literary life.

One of the myths about Fitzgerald, a myth he sometimes encouraged, was that he was quick and facile and that composition came easily to him. His manuscripts and typescripts tell a different story. He was rarely able to produce good writing spontaneously; usually he arrived at a publishable text only after much revising, cutting, polishing, and recasting. Preserved among his papers at Princeton are manuscripts and typescripts for most of the items in this collection. These documents testify to the work that Fitzgerald put into these pieces. For example, five typescripts in two different versions are extant for "Author's House"; three variant typescripts survive for "Afternoon of an Author"; six typescripts, all bearing handwritten revisions, are preserved for "My Generation." Fitzgerald took pains with these pieces and released them for print only after much literary labor.

Fitzgerald's life ran parallel to the peaks and dips and spasms of American society. For him the 1910s were a hopeful time of striving and idealism; the 1920s were boom years filled with new pleasures; the 1930s were an extended period of reflection and retrenchment. He would have captured all of that in a personal memoir. If he had lived into the 1940s he would have had a great deal to say about that decade as well—a period during which his country went through a second great war, very different from the one in which he and his college classmates had participated. A memoir by Fitzgerald would have been a brilliant performance, comparable to Gertrude Stein's *The Autobiography of Alice B. Toklas* and Ernest Hemingway's *A Moveable Feast*. It's regrettable that Fitzgerald did not write such a book, but he did leave behind a substantial body of personal writing, from which the items in this collection have been taken. His writings about his own life retain their bite and freshness; they teach important lessons and offer insights into his professionalism and his genius.

J.L.W.W. III

Quotations in this preface are taken from Fitzgerald to Perkins, May 15, 1934, and April 2, 1936, and from Perkins to Fitzgerald, March 26, 1936. These letters are published in *Dear Scott/Dear Max: The Fitzgerald-Perkins Correspondence*, ed. John Kuehl and Jackson R. Bryer (New York: Scribner's, 1971), 197, 228–29.

Textual Note

The texts for fifteen of the nineteen items in this collection are taken from *My Lost City: Personal Essays, 1920–1940*, a volume in the Cambridge Edition of the Works of F. Scott Fitzgerald published in 2005 by Cambridge University Press. The texts in the Cambridge series have been newly established from original manuscripts, typescripts, and other materials in the Fitzgerald Papers at Princeton University Library. Passages excised by magazine editors for reasons of space have been restored. Fitzgerald's characteristic pointing and word division have been followed, including his habit of occasionally omitting the comma that divides the two clauses of a compound sentence, his inconsistent use of the final comma in a series, and his habit of placing titles of books, newspapers, and other publications within quotation marks in order to reserve italics for emphasis. A full record of textual variants is included in the Cambridge volume, together with extensive explanatory notes, from which the annotations in the present volume are drawn. The texts of "An Interview with Mr. Fitzgerald," "Three Cities," "Salesmanship in the Champs-Élysées," and "The Death of My Father" have been taken from their first periodical appearances.

A Short
Autobiography

A SHORT
AUTOBIOGRAPHY

Who's Who—and Why

The history of my life is the history of the struggle between an overwhelming urge to write and a combination of circumstances bent on keeping me from it.

When I lived in St. Paul and was about twelve I wrote all through every class in school in the back of my geography book and first year Latin and on the margins of themes and declensions and mathematic problems. Two years later a family congress decided that the only way to force me to study was to send me to boarding school. This was a mistake. It took my mind off my writing. I decided to play football, to smoke, to go to college, to do all sorts of irrelevant things that had nothing to do with the real business of life, which, of course, was the proper mixture of description and dialogue in the short story.

But in school I went off on a new tack. I saw a musical comedy called "The Quaker Girl," and from that day forth my desk bulged with Gilbert & Sullivan librettos and dozens of notebooks containing the germs of dozens of musical comedies.

Near the end of my last year at school I came across a new musical-comedy score lying on top of the piano. It was a show called "His Honor the Sultan," and the title furnished the information that it had been presented by the Triangle Club of Princeton University.

That was enough for me. From then on the university question was settled. I was bound for Princeton.

I spent my entire freshman year writing an operetta for the Triangle Club. To do this I failed in algebra, trigonometry, coördinate geometry and hygiene. But the Triangle Club accepted my show, and by tutoring all through a stuffy August I managed to come back a sophomore and act in it as a chorus girl. A little after this came a hiatus. My health broke down and I left college one December to spend the rest of the year recuperating in the West. Almost my final memory before I left was of writing a last lyric on that year's Triangle production while in bed in the infirmary with a high fever.

The next year, 1916–17, found me back in college, but by this time I had decided that poetry was the only thing worth while, so with my head ringing with the meters of Swinburne and the matters of Rupert Brooke I spent the spring doing sonnets, ballads and rondels into the small hours. I had read somewhere that every great poet had written great poetry before he was twenty-one. I had only a year and, besides, war was impending. I must publish a book of startling verse before I was engulfed.

By autumn I was in an infantry officers' training camp at Fort Leavenworth, with poetry in the discard and a brand-new ambition—I was writing an immortal novel. Every evening, concealing my pad behind "Small Problems for Infantry," I wrote paragraph after paragraph on a somewhat edited history of me and my imagination. The outline of twenty-two chapters, four of them in verse, was made; two chapters were completed; and then I was detected and the game was up. I could write no more during study period.

This was a distinct complication. I had only three months to live—in those days all infantry officers thought they had only three months to live—and I had left no mark on the world. But such consuming ambition was not to be thwarted by a mere war. Every Saturday at one o'clock when the week's work was over I hurried to the Officers' Club, and there, in a corner of a roomful of smoke, conversation and rattling newspapers, I wrote a one-hundred-and-twenty-thousand-word novel on the consecutive week-ends of three months. There was no revising; there was no time for it. As I finished each chapter I sent it to a typist in Princeton.

Meanwhile I lived in its smeary pencil pages. The drills, marches and "Small Problems for Infantry" were a shadowy dream. My whole heart was concentrated upon my book.

I went to my regiment happy. I had written a novel. The war could now go on. I forgot paragraphs and pentameters, similes and syllogisms. I got to be a first lieutenant, got my orders overseas—and then the publishers wrote me that though "The Romantic Egotist" was the most original manuscript they had received for years they couldn't publish it. It was crude and reached no conclusion.

It was six months after this that I arrived in New York and presented my card to the office boys of seven city editors asking to be taken on as a reporter. I had just turned twenty-two, the war was over, and I was going to trail murderers by day and do short stories by night. But the newspapers didn't need me. They sent their office boys out to tell me they didn't need me. They decided definitely and irrevocably by the sound of my name on a calling card that I was absolutely unfitted to be a reporter.

Instead I became an advertising man at ninety dollars a month, writing the slogans that while away the weary hours in rural trolley cars. After hours I wrote stories—from March to June. There were nineteen altogether, the quickest written in an hour and a half, the slowest in three days. No one bought them, no one sent personal letters. I had one hundred and twenty-two rejection slips pinned in a frieze about my room. I wrote movies. I wrote song lyrics. I wrote complicated advertising schemes. I wrote poems. I wrote sketches. I wrote jokes. Near the end of June I sold one story for thirty dollars.

On the Fourth of July, utterly disgusted with myself and all the editors, I went home to St. Paul and informed family and friends that I had given up my position and had come home to write a novel. They nodded politely, changed the subject and spoke of me very gently. But this time I knew what I was doing. I had a novel to write at last, and all through two hot months I wrote and revised and compiled and boiled down. On September fifteenth "This Side of Paradise" was accepted by special delivery.

In the next two months I wrote eight stories and sold nine. The ninth was accepted by the same magazine that had rejected it four months before. Then, in November, I sold my first story to the editors of the "Saturday Evening Post." By February I had sold them half a dozen. Then my novel came out. Then I got married. Now I spend my time wondering how it all happened.

In the words of the immortal Julius Caesar: "That's all there is; there isn't any more."

—*Saturday Evening Post,* September 18, 1920

An Interview with Mr. Fitzgerald
by F. Scott Fitzgerald

With the distinct intention of taking Mr. Fitzgerald by surprise I ascended to the twenty-first floor of the Biltmore and knocked in the best waiter-manner at the door. On entering my first impression was one of confusion—a sort of rummage sale confusion. A young man was standing in the center of the room turning an absent glance first at one side of the room and then at the other.

"I'm looking for my hat," he said dazedly. "How do you do. Come on in and sit on the bed."

The author of *This Side of Paradise* is sturdy, broad-shouldered and just above medium height. He has blond hair with the suggestion of a wave and alert green eyes—the mélange somewhat Nordic—and good-looking too, which was disconcerting as I had somehow expected a thin nose and spectacles.

We had preliminaries—but I will omit the preliminaries. They consisted in searching for things: cigarettes, a blue tie with white dots, an ash tray. But as he was obviously quite willing to talk, and seemed quite receptive to my questions, we launched off directly on his ideas of literature.

"How long did it take to write your book?" I began.

"To write it—three months, to conceive it—three minutes. To collect the data in it—all my life. The idea of writing it occurred to me on the first of last July. It was sort of a substitute form of dissipation."

"What are your plans now?" I asked him.

He gave a long sigh and shrugged his shoulders.

"I'll be darned if I know. The scope and depth and breadth of my writings lie in the laps of the gods. If knowledge comes naturally, through interest, as Shaw learned his political economy or as Wells devoured modern science—why, that'll be slick. On study itself—that is in 'reading up' a subject—I haven't anthill-moving faith. Knowledge must cry out to be known—cry out that only I can know it, and then I'll swim in it to satiety as I've swum in—in many things."

"Please be frank."

"Well, you know if you've read my book. I've swum in various seas of adolescent egotism. But what I meant was that if big things never grip me—well, it simply means I'm not cut out to be big. This conscious struggle to find bigness outside, to substitute bigness of theme for bigness of perception, to create an objective *magnum opus* such as *The Ring and the Book*—well, all that's the antithesis of my literary aims.

"Another thing," he continued. "My idea is always to reach my generation. The wise writer, I think, writes for the youth of his own generation, the critic of the next and the schoolmasters of ever afterward. Granted the ability to improve what he imitates in the way of style, to choose from his own interpretation of the experiences around him what constitutes material, and we get the first-water genius."

"Do you expect to be—to be—well, part of the great literary tradition?" I asked, timidly.

He became excited. He smiled radiantly. I saw he had an answer for this. "There's no great literary tradition," he burst out. "There's only the tradition of the eventual death of every literary tradition. The wise literary son kills his own father."

After this he began enthusiastically on style.

"By style, I mean color," he said. "I want to be able to do anything with words: handle slashing, flaming descriptions like Wells, and use the paradox with the clarity of Samuel Butler, the breadth of Bernard Shaw and the wit of Oscar Wilde. I want to do the wide sultry heavens of Conrad, the rolled-gold sundowns and crazy-quilt skies of Hichens and Kipling as well as the pastel dawns and twilights of Chesterton. All that is by way of example. As a matter of fact I am a professed literary thief, hot after the best methods of every writer in my generation."

The interview terminated about then. Four young men with philistine faces and conservative ties appeared and, looking at each other, exchanged broad winks. Mr. Fitzgerald faltered and seemed to lose his stride.

"Most of my friends are—are like those," he whispered as he showed me to the door. "I don't care for literary people much—they make me nervous."

It was really rather a good interview, wasn't it!

—*Saturday Review*, November 5, 1960

Fitzgerald concocted this self-interview in the spring of 1920, a few weeks after the publication of *This Side of Paradise*, when the novel (and its author) were much in the public eye. The Scribner's publicity department sent the interview to the book critic Heywood Broun, who quoted from it in his "Books" column in the *New York Tribune* (May 7, 1920). The entire text of the interview was published, from Fitzgerald's manuscript, in the *Saturday Review*, November 5, 1960. That text is published here.

Three Cities

It began in Paris, that impression—fleeting, chiefly literary, unprofound—that the world was growing darker. We carefully reconstructed an old theory and, blond both of us, cast supercilious Nordic glances at the play of the dark children around us. We had left America less than one half of one per cent American, but the pernicious and sentimental sap was destined to rise again within us. We boiled with ancient indignations toward the French. We sat in front of Anatole France's house for an hour in hope of seeing the old gentleman come out—but we thought simultaneously that when he dies, the France of flame and glory dies with him. We drove in the Bois de Boulogne—thinking of France as a spoiled and revengeful child which, having kept Europe in a turmoil for two hundred years, has spent the last forty demanding assistance in its battles, that the continent may be kept as much like a bloody sewer as possible.

In Brentano's near the Café de la Paix, I picked up Dreiser's suppressed "Genius" for three dollars. With the exception of "The Titan" I liked it best among his five novels, in spite of the preposterous Christian Science episode near the end. We stayed in Paris long enough to finish it.

Italy, which is to the English what France is to the Americans, was in a pleasant humor. As a French comedy writer remarked we inevitably detest our benefactors,

8

so I was glad to see that Italy was casting off four years of unhealthy suppressed desires. In Florence you could hardly blame a squad of Italian soldiers for knocking down an Omaha lady who was unwilling to give up her compartment to a Colonel. Why, the impudent woman could not speak Italian! So the *Carabinieri* can hardly be blamed for being incensed. And as for knocking her around a little—well, boys will be boys. The American ambassadorial tradition in Rome having for some time been in the direct line of sentimental American literature, I do not doubt that even they found some compensating sweetness in the natures of the naughty *Bersaglieri*.

We were in Rome two weeks. You can see the fascination of the place. We stayed two weeks even though we could have left in two days—that is we *could* have left if we had not run out of money. I met John Carter, the author of "These Wild Young People," in the street one day and he cashed me a check for a thousand lira. We spent this on ointment. The ointment trust thrives in Rome. All the guests at the two best hotels are afflicted with what the proprietors call "mosquitoes too small for screens." We do not call them that in America.

John Carter lent us "Alice Adams" and we read it aloud to each other under the shadow of Caesar's house. If it had not been for Alice we should have collapsed and died in Rome as so many less fortunate literary people have done. "Alice Adams" more than atones for the childish heroics of "Ramsey Milholland" and for the farcical spiritualism in "The Magnificent Ambersons." After having made three brave attempts to struggle through "Moon-Calf" it was paradise to read someone who knows how to write.

By bribing the ticket agent with one thousand lira to cheat some old General out of his compartment—the offer was the agent's, not ours—we managed to leave Italy.

"Vous avez quelque chose pour déclarer?" asked the border customs officials early next morning (only they asked it in better French).

I awoke with a horrible effort from a dream of Italian beggars.

"Oui!" I shrieked. *"Je veux déclare que je suis très, très heureux a partir d'Italie!"* I could understand at last why the French loved France. They have seen Italy.

We had been to Oxford before—after Italy we went back there, arriving gorgeously at twilight when the place was fully peopled for us by the ghosts of ghosts—the characters, romantic, absurd or melancholy, of "Sinister Street," "Zuleika Dobson" and "Jude the Obscure." But something was wrong now—something that would never be right again. Here was Rome—here on The High were the shadows of the Via Appia. In how many years would our descendents approach this ruin with supercilious eyes to buy postcards from men of a short, inferior race—a race that once were Englishmen. How soon—for money follows the rich lands and the healthy stock, and art follows begging after money. Your time will come, New York, fifty years, sixty. Apollo's head is peering crazily, in new colors that our generation will never live to know, over the tip of the next century.

—*Brentano's Book Chat,* September–October 1921

What I Think and Feel at 25

The man stopped me on the street. He was ancient, but not a mariner. He had a long beard and a glittering eye. I think he was a friend of the family's, or something.

"Say, Fitzgerald," he said, "say! Will you tell me this: What in the blinkety-blank-blank has a—has a man of your age got to go saying these pessimistic things for? What's the idea?" I tried to laugh him off. He told me that he and my grandfather had been boys together. After that, I had no wish to corrupt him. So I tried to laugh him off.

"Ha-ha-ha!" I said determinedly. "Ha-ha-ha!" And then I added, "Ha-ha! Well, I'll see you later."

With this I attempted to pass him by, but he seized my arm firmly and showed symptoms of spending the afternoon in my company.

"When I was a boy—" he began, and then he drew the picture that people always draw of what excellent, happy, care-free souls they were at twenty-five. That is, he told me all the things he liked to *think* he thought in the misty past.

I allowed him to continue. I even made polite grunts at intervals to express my astonishment. For I will be doing it myself some day. I will concoct for my juniors a Scott Fitzgerald that, it's safe to say, none of my contemporaries would at present recognize. But they will be old themselves then; and they will respect my concoction as I shall respect theirs. . . .

"And now," the happy ancient was concluding, "you are young, you have good health, you have made money, you are exceptionally happily married, you have achieved considerable success while you are still young enough to enjoy it—will you tell an innocent old man just why you write those—"

I succumbed. I would tell him. I began:

"Well, you see, sir, it seems to me that as a man gets older he grows more vulner—"

But I got no further. As soon as I began to talk he hurriedly shook my hand and departed. He did not want to listen. He did not care why I thought what I thought. He had simply felt the need of giving a little speech, and I had been the victim. His receding form disappeared with a slight wobble around the next corner.

"All right, you old bore," I muttered; "*don't* listen, then. You wouldn't understand, anyhow." I took an awful kick at a curbstone, as a sort of proxy, and continued my walk.

Now, that's the first incident. The second was when a man came to me not long ago from a big newspaper syndicate, and said:

"Mr. Fitzgerald, there's a rumor around New York that you and—ah—you and Mrs. Fitzgerald are going to commit suicide at thirty because you hate and dread middle age. I want to give you some publicity in this matter by getting it up as a story for the feature sections of five hundred and fourteen Sunday newspapers. In one corner of the page will be—"

"Don't!" I cried. "I know: In one corner will stand the doomed couple, she with an arsenic sundae, he with an Oriental dagger. Both of them will have their eyes fixed on a large clock, on the face of which will be a skull and crossbones. In the other corner will be a big calendar with the date marked in red."

"That's it!" cried the syndicate man enthusiastically. "You've grasped the idea. Now, what we—"

"Listen here!" I said severely. "There is nothing in that rumor. Nothing whatever. When I'm thirty I won't be *this* me—I'll be somebody else. I'll have a different body, because it said so in a book I read once, and I'll have a different attitude on everything. I'll even be married to a different person—"

"Ah!" he interrupted, with an eager light in his eye, and produced a notebook. "That's very interesting."

"No, no, no!" I cried hastily. "I mean my wife will be different."

"I see. You plan a divorce."

"No! I mean—"

"Well, it's all the same. Now, what we want, in order to fill out this story, is a lot of remarks about petting-parties. Do you think the—ah—petting-party is a serious menace to the Constitution? And, just to link it up, can we say that your suicide will be largely on account of past petting-parties?"

"See here!" I interrupted in despair. "Try to understand. I don't know what petting-parties have to do with the question. I have always dreaded age, because it invariably increases the vulner—"

But, as in the case of the family friend, I got no further. The syndicate man grasped my hand firmly. He shook it. Then he muttered something about interviewing a chorus girl who was reported to have an anklet of solid platinum, and hurried off.

That's the second incident. You see, I had managed to tell two different men that "age increased the vulner—" But they had not been interested. The old man had talked about himself and the syndicate man had talked about petting-parties. When I began to talk about the "vulner—" they both had sudden engagements.

So, with one hand on the Eighteenth Amendment and the other hand on the serious part of the Constitution, I have taken an oath that I will tell somebody my story.

As a man grows older it stands to reason that his vulnerability increases. Three years ago, for instance, I could be hurt in only one way—through myself. If my best friend's wife had her hair torn off by an electric washing-machine, I was grieved, of course. I would make my friend a long speech full of "old mans," and finish up with a paragraph from Washington's Farewell Address; but when I'd finished I could go to a good restaurant and enjoy my dinner as usual. If my second cousin's husband had an artery severed while having his nails manicured, I will not deny that it was a matter of considerable regret to me. But when I heard the news I did *not* faint and have to be taken home in a passing laundry wagon.

In fact I was pretty much invulnerable. I put up a conventional wail whenever a ship was sunk or a train got wrecked; but I don't suppose, if the whole city of Chicago had been wiped out, I'd have lost a night's sleep over it—unless something led me to believe that St. Paul was the next city on the list. Even then I could have moved my luggage over to Minneapolis and rested pretty comfortably all night.

But that was three years ago when I was still a young man. I was only twenty-two. When I said anything the book reviewers didn't like, they could say, "Gosh! That certainly is callow!" And that finished me. Label it "callow," and that was enough.

Well, now I'm twenty-five I'm not callow any longer—at least not so that I can notice it when I look in an ordinary mirror. Instead, I'm vulnerable. I'm vulnerable in every way.

For the benefit of revenue agents and moving-picture directors who may be reading this magazine I will explain that vulnerable means easily wounded. Well, that's it. I'm more easily wounded. I can not only be wounded in the chest, the feelings, the teeth, the bank account; but I can be wounded in the *dog*. Do I make myself clear? In the dog.

No, that isn't a new part of the body just discovered by the Rockefeller Institute. I mean a real dog. I mean if anyone gives my family dog to the dog-catcher he's hurting *me* almost as much as he's hurting the dog. He's hurting me *in* the dog. And if our doctor says to me tomorrow, "That child of yours isn't going to be a blonde after all," well, he's wounded me in a way I couldn't have been wounded in before, because I never before had a child to be wounded in. And if my daughter grows up and when she's sixteen elopes with some fellow from Zion City who believes the world is flat—I wouldn't write this except that she's only six months old and can't quite read yet, so it won't put any ideas in her head—why, then I'll be wounded again.

About being wounded through your wife I will not enter into, as it is a delicate subject. I will not say anything about my case. But I have private reasons for knowing that if anybody said to your wife one day that it was a shame she *would* wear yellow when it made her look so peaked, you would suffer violently, within six hours afterward, for what that person said.

"Attack him through his wife!" "Kidnap his child!" "Tie a tin can to his dog's tail!" How often do we hear those slogans in life, not to mention in the movies. And how they make me wince! Three years ago, you could have yelled them outside my window all through a summer night, and I wouldn't have batted an eye. The only thing that would have aroused me would have been: "Wait a minute. I think I can pot him from here."

I used to have about ten square feet of skin vulnerable

to chills and fevers. Now I have about twenty. I have not personally enlarged—the twenty feet includes the skin of my family—but I might as well have, because if a chill or fever strikes any bit of that twenty feet of skin *I* begin to shiver.

And so I ooze gently into middle age; for the true middle age is not the acquirement of years, but the acquirement of a family. The incomes of the childless have wonderful elasticity. Two people require a room and a bath; couple with child requires the millionaire's suite on the sunny side of the hotel.

So let me start the religious part of this article by saying that if the Editor thought he was going to get something young and happy—yes, and callow—I have got to refer him to my daughter, if she will give dictation. If anybody thinks that I am callow they ought to see her—she's so callow it makes me laugh. It even makes her laugh, too, to think how callow she is. If any literary critics saw her they'd have a nervous breakdown right on the spot. But, on the other hand, anybody writing to me, an editor or anybody else, is writing to a middle-aged man.

Well, I'm twenty-five, and I have to admit that I'm pretty well satisfied with *some* of that time. That is to say, the first five years seemed to go all right—but the last twenty! They have been a matter of violently contrasted extremes. In fact, this has struck me so forcibly that from time to time I have kept charts, trying to figure out the years when I was closest to happy. Then I get mad and tear up the charts.

Skipping that long list of mistakes which passes for my boyhood I will say that I went away to preparatory school at fifteen, and that my two years there were wasted, were years of utter and profitless unhappiness. I was unhappy because I was cast into a situation where everybody thought I ought to behave just as they behaved—and I didn't have the courage to shut up and go my own way, anyhow.

For example, there was a rather dull boy at school named Percy, whose approval, I felt, for some unfathomable reason, I must have. So, for the sake of this negligible cipher, I started out to let as much of my mind as I had under mild cultivation sink back into a state of heavy underbrush. I spent hours in a damp gymnasium fooling around with a muggy basket-ball and working myself into a damp, muggy rage, when I wanted, instead, to go walking in the country.

And all this to please Percy. He thought it was the thing to do. If you didn't go through the damp business every day you were "morbid." That was his favorite word, and it had me frightened. I didn't want to be morbid. So I became muggy instead.

Besides, Percy was dull in classes; so I used to pretend to be dull also. When I wrote stories I wrote them secretly, and felt like a criminal. If I gave birth to any idea that did not appeal to Percy's pleasant, vacant mind I discarded the idea at once and felt like apologizing.

Of course Percy never got into college. He went to work and I have scarcely seen him since, though I understand that he has since become an undertaker of considerable standing. The time I spent with him was wasted; but, worse than that, I did not enjoy the wasting of it. At least, he had nothing to give me, and I had not the faintest reasons for caring what he thought or said. But when I discovered this it was too late.

The worst of it is that this same business went on until I was twenty-two. That is, I'd be perfectly happy doing just what I wanted to do, when somebody would begin shaking his head and saying:

"Now see here, Fitzgerald, you mustn't go on doing that. It's—it's morbid."

And I was always properly awed by the word "morbid," so I quit what I wanted to do and what it was good for me to do, and did what some other fellow wanted me to do. Every once in awhile, though, I used to tell somebody to go to the devil; otherwise I never would have done anything at all.

In officers' training camp during 1917 I started to write a novel. I would begin work at it every Saturday afternoon at one and work like mad until midnight. Then I would work at it from six Sunday morning until six Sunday night, when I had to report back to barracks. I was thoroughly enjoying myself.

After a month three friends came to me with scowling faces:

"See here, Fitzgerald, you ought to use the weekends in getting some good rest and recreation. The way you use them is—is morbid!"

That word convinced me. It sent the usual shiver down my spine. The next weekend I laid the novel aside, went into town with the others and danced all night at a party. But I began to worry about my novel. I worried so much that I returned to camp, not rested, but utterly miserable. I *was* morbid then. But I never went to town again. I finished the novel. It was rejected; but a year later I rewrote it and it was published under the title "This Side of Paradise."

But before I rewrote it I had a list of "morbids," chalked up against people that, placed end to end, would have reached to the nearest lunatic asylum. It was morbid:

1st. To get engaged without enough money to marry
2d. To leave the advertising business after three months
3d. To want to write at all
4th. To think I could
5th. To write about "silly little boys and girls that nobody wants to read about."

And so on, until a year later, when I found to my surprise that everybody had been only kidding—they had believed all their lives that writing was the only thing for me, and had hardly been able to keep from telling me all the time.

But I am really not old enough to begin drawing morals out of my own life to elevate the young. I will save that pastime until I am sixty; and then, as I have said, I will concoct a Scott Fitzgerald who will make Benjamin Franklin look like a lucky devil who loafed into prominence. Even in the above account I have managed to sketch the outline of a small but neat halo. I take it all back. I am twenty-five years old. I wish I had ten million dollars, and never had to do another lick of work as long as I live.

But as I *do* have to keep at it, I might as well declare that the chief thing I've learned so far is: If you don't know much—well, nobody else knows much more. And nobody knows half as much about your own interests as *you* know.

If you believe in anything very strongly—including yourself—and if you go after that thing alone, you end up in jail, in heaven, in the headlines, or in the largest house in the block, according to what you started after. If you *don't* believe in anything very strongly—including yourself—you go along, and enough money is made out of you to buy an automobile for some other fellow's son, and you marry if you've got time, and if you do you have a lot of children, whether you have time or not, and finally you get tired and you die.

If you're in the second of those two classes you have the most fun before you're twenty-five. If you're in the first, you have it afterward.

You see, if you're in the first class you'll frequently be called a darn fool—or worse. That was as true in Philadelphia about 1727 as it is today. Anybody knows that a kid that walked around town munching a loaf of bread and not caring what anybody thought was a darn fool. It stands to reason! But there are a lot of darn fools who get their pictures in the schoolbooks—with their names under the pictures. And the sensible fellows, the ones that had time to laugh, well, their pictures are in there, too. But their *names* aren't—and the laughs look sort of frozen on their faces.

The particular sort of darn fool I mean ought to remember that he's *least* a darn fool when he's being *called* a darn fool. The main thing is to be your own kind of a darn fool.

(The above advice is of course only for darn fools *under* twenty-five. It may be all wrong for darn fools over twenty-five.)

I don't know why it is that when I start to write about being twenty-five I suddenly begin to write about darn fools. I do not see any connection. Now, if I were asked to write about darn fools, I would write about people who have their front teeth filled with gold, because a friend of mine did that the other day, and after being mistaken for a jewelry store three times in one hour he came up and asked me if I thought it showed too much. As I am a kind man, I told him I would not have noticed it if the sun hadn't been so strong on it. I asked him why he had it done.

"Well," he said, "the dentist told me a porcelain filling never lasted more than ten years."

"Ten years! Why, you may be dead in ten years."

"That's true."

"Of course it'll be nice that all the time you're in your coffin you'll never have to worry about your teeth."

And it occurred to me that about half the people in the world are always having their front teeth filled with gold. That is, they're figuring on twenty years from now. Well, when you're young it's all right figuring your success a long ways ahead—if you don't make it *too* long. But as for your pleasure—your front teeth!—it's better to figure on today.

And that's the second thing I learned while getting vulnerable and middle-aged. Let me recapitulate:

1st. I think that compared to what you know about your own business nobody else knows *any*thing. And if anybody knows more about it than you do, then it's *his* business and you're *his* man, not your own. And as soon as your business becomes *your* business you'll know more about it than anybody else.

2d. Never have your front teeth filled with gold.

And now I will stop pretending to be a pleasant young fellow and disclose my real nature. I will prove to you, if you have not found it out already, that I have a mean streak and nobody would like to have me for a son.

I do not like old people. They are always talking about their "experience"—and very few of them have any. In fact, most of them go on making the same mistakes at fifty and believing in the same white list of approved twenty-carat lies that they did at seventeen. And it all starts with my old friend vulnerability.

Take a woman of thirty. She is considered lucky if she has allied herself to a multitude of things: her husband, her children, her home, her servant. If she has three homes, eight children, and fourteen servants, she is considered luckier still. (This, of course, does not generally apply to more husbands.)

Now, when she was young she worried only about herself; but now she must be worried by *any* trouble occurring to *any* of these people or things. She is ten times as vulnerable. Moreover, she can never break one of these ties or relieve herself of one of these burdens except at the cost of great pain and sorrow to herself. They are the things that break her, and yet they are the most precious things in life.

In consequence, everything which doesn't go to make her secure, or at least to give her a sense of security, startles and annoys her. She acquires only the useless knowledge found in cheap movies, cheap novels, and the cheap memoirs of titled foreigners.

By this time her husband also has become suspicious of anything gay or new. He seldom addresses her, except in a series of profound grunts, or to ask whether she has sent his shirts out to the laundry. At the family dinner on Sunday he occasionally gives her some fascinating statistics on party politics, some opinions from that morning's newspaper editorial.

But after thirty, both husband and wife know in their hearts that the game is up. Without a few cocktails social intercourse becomes a torment. It is no longer spontaneous; it is a convention by which they agree to shut their eyes to the fact that the other men and women they know are tired and dull and fat, and yet must be put up with as politely as they themselves are put up with in their turn.

I have seen many happy young couples—but I have seldom seen a happy home after husband and wife are thirty. Most homes can be divided into four classes:

1st. Where the husband is a pretty conceited guy who thinks that a dinky insurance business is a lot harder than raising babies, and that everybody ought to kow-tow to him at home. He is the kind whose sons usually get away from home as soon as they can walk.

2d. When the wife has got a sharp tongue and the martyr complex, and thinks she's the only woman in the world that ever had a child. This is probably the unhappiest home of all.

3d. Where the children are always being reminded how nice it was of the parents to bring them into the world, and how they ought to respect their parents for being born in 1870 instead of 1902.

4th. Where everything is for the children. Where the parents pay much more for the children's education than they can afford, and spoil them unreasonably. This usually ends by the children being ashamed of the parents.

And yet I think that marriage is the most satisfactory institution we have. I'm simply stating my belief that when Life has used us for its purposes it takes away all our attractive qualities and gives us, instead, ponderous but shallow convictions of our own wisdom and "experience."

Needless to say, as old people run the world, an enormous camouflage has been built up to hide the fact that only young people are attractive or important.

Having got in wrong with many of the readers of this article, I will now proceed to close. If you don't agree with me on any minor points you have a right to say: "Gosh! He certainly is callow!" and turn to something else. Personally I do not consider that I am callow, because I do not see how anybody of my age could be callow. For instance, I was reading an article in this magazine a few months ago by a fellow named Ring Lardner that says he is thirty-five, and it seemed to me how young and happy and carefree he was in comparison with me.

Maybe he is vulnerable, too. He did not say so. Maybe when you get to be thirty-five you do not *know* any more how vulnerable you *are*. All I can say is that if he ever gets to be twenty-five again, which is very unlikely, maybe he will agree with me. The older I grow the more I get so I don't know anything. If I had been asked to do this article about five years ago it might have been worth reading.

—*American Magazine*, September 1922

Imagination—
and a Few Mothers

Back in the days of tenement uplift, the homes of tired
stevedores and banana peddlers were frequently invaded
by pompous dowagers who kept their limousines purr-
ing at the curb. "Giuseppi," say the pompous dowagers,
"what you need to brighten up your home is a game of
charades every evening."

"Charade?" inquires the bewildered Giuseppi.

"Family charades," beam the dowagers. "For instance,
suppose some night your wife and the girls take the name
'Viscountess Salisbury,' or the words 'initiative and refer-
endum,' and act them out—and you and the boys can
guess what words they're acting. So much more real fun
than the saloon."

Having sown the good seed, the dowagers reenter their
limousines and drive to the next Giuseppi on their list,
a list made out by the Society for Encouraging Parlor
Games in Poor Families.

Thus went the attempt from on high to bring imagination into the home, an attempt about as successful as the
current effort to clothe the native Hawaiians in dollar-
eighty-five cheesecloth Mother Hubbards manufactured
in Paterson, New Jersey.

The average home is a horribly dull place. This is a
platitude; it's so far taken for granted that it's the basis of

much of our national humor. The desire of the man for the club and the wife for the movie—as Shelley did *not* put it—has recently been supplemented by the cry of the child for the moonlight ride.

The statistics compiled last year by the state of Arkansas show that of every one hundred wives thirty-seven admit that they married chiefly to get away from home. The figures are appalling. That nineteen of the thirty-seven wished themselves home again as soon as they were married does not mitigate the frightful situation.

It is easy to say that the home fails chiefly in imagination. But an imagination under good control is about as rare a commodity as radium, and does not consist of playing charades or giving an imitation of Charlie Chaplin or putting papier-mâché shades on the 1891 gas jets; imagination is an attitude toward living. It is a putting into the terrific, life-long, age-old fight against domestic dullness all the energy that goes into worry and self-justification and nagging, which are the pet devices of all of us for whiling away the heavy hours.

The word energy at once brings up the picture of a big, bustling woman, breathing hard through closed lips, rushing from child to child and trying to organize a dear little Christmas play in the parlor. But that isn't at all the kind of imagination I mean.

There are several kinds. For example, I once knew the mother of a family, a Mrs. Judkins, who had a marvelous imagination. If things had been a little different, Mrs. Judkins might have sold her imagination to the movies or the magazines, or invented a new kind of hook-and-eye. Or she might have put it into that intricate and delicate business of running a successful home. Did Mrs. Judkins use her imagination for these things? She did not! She had none left to use.

Her imagination had a leak in it, and its stuff was dissipated hourly into thin air—in this fashion: At six A.M. Mrs. Judkins awakes. She lies in bed. She begins her daily worry. Did, or did not, her daughter Anita look tired last night when she came in from that dance? Yes; she did. She had dark circles. Dark circles—a bogey of her childhood. Mrs. Judkins remembers how her own mother always worried about dark circles. Without doubt Anita is going into a nervous decline. How ghastly! Think of that Mrs.—what was her name?—who had the nervous decline at—at—what was that place? Think of it! Appalling! Well, I'll—I'll ask her to go to a doctor; but what if she won't go? Maybe I can get her to stay home from dances for—for a month.

Out of her bed springs Mrs. Judkins in a state of nervous worry. She is impelled by a notion of doing some vague, nervous thing to avoid some vague, nervous catastrophe. She is already fatigued, because she should have gone back to sleep for an hour; but sleep is now out of the question. Her wonderful imagination has conjured up Anita's lapse into a bed of pain, her last words—something about "going back to the angels"—and her pitiful extinction.

Anita, who is seventeen and a healthy, hardy flapper, has merely plunged healthily and hardily into having a good time. For two nights in succession she has been out late at dances. The second night she was tired and developed dark circles. Today she will sleep until twelve o'clock, if Mrs. Judkins doesn't wake her to ask her how she feels, and will get up looking like a magazine cover.

But it is only eight o'clock now, and we must return to Mrs. Judkins. She has tiptoed in to look at the doomed Anita, and on her way has glanced into the room where sleeps Clifford Judkins, third, age twelve. Her imagination is now running at fever heat. It is started for the day and will pulsate at the rate of sixty vivid images a minute until she falls into a weary coma at one o'clock tonight.

So she endows Clifford with dark circles also.

Poor Clifford! She decides not to wake him for school. He's not strong enough. She'll write a note to his teacher and explain. He looked tired yesterday when he came in from playing baseball. Baseball! Another ghastly thought! Why, suppose—

But I will not depress you by taking you through all the early hours of Mrs. Judkins' morning; because she *is* depressing. A human being in a nervous, worried state is one of the most depressing things in the world. Mrs. Judkins is exhausted already so far as having the faintest cheerful effect on anyone else is concerned. In fact, after breakfast Mr. Judkins leaves the house with the impression that things are going pretty badly at home and that life's a pretty dismal proposition.

But before he left he did a very unfortunate thing. Something in the newspaper made him exclaim that if they passed that Gunch-Bobly tariff law his business was going to the dogs. It was merely a conventional grumble. Complaining about the Gunch-Bobly tariff law is his pet hobby, but—

He has put a whole bag of grist—does grist come in bags?—into the mill of Mrs. Judkins' imagination. By the time he reaches the street car Mrs. Judkins has got him into bankruptcy. By the time he is downtown he has—though he doesn't know it—been spending a year in prison, with a woman and two starving children calling for him outside the gates. When he enters his office he is unconsciously entering the poorhouse, there to weep out a miserable old age.

But enough; a few more hours of Mrs. Judkins' day would exhaust me and you, as it exhausts everybody with whom she comes into contact.

There are many Mrs. Judkinses, and I could go on forever. But I will spare you, for I want to talk about one woman who together with several others I know fought the good fight against the dullness and boredom of the home and, by an unusual device, won a triumphant and deserved victory.

I'm going to tell you about a charming woman who, as I have said, used her imagination in an unusual way. Hers was the happiest home I ever knew.

Did she work for awhile in her husband's office and learn how his business was run, so that she could talk to him about it in the evenings? Reader, she did not. Did she buy a football guide and master the rules so that she could discuss the game understandingly with her sons? No; she didn't. Nor did she organize a family orchestra in which Clarence played the drum, Maisee the harp and Vivian the oboe. She knew nothing about football, nor did she ever intend to. Her remarks on her husband's business were delightfully vague. He was a manufacturer of stationery, and I think that in some confused way she imagined that he ran the Post Office Department.

No; she was not one of those appalling women who know more about the business of everybody in the house than anyone knows about his own. She never bored her boys by instructing them in football, though she occasionally delighted them by her ludicrous misapprehensions of how it was played. And she never dragged the paper industry onto the domestic hearth. She couldn't even solve her own daughter's algebra problems; she admitted it and didn't try. In fact, she was not at all the model mother, as mapped out by Miss Emily Hope Demster, of the Wayondotte Valley Normal School, in her paper on Keeping Ahead of Your Children.

She used her imagination in a finer and more far-seeing way. She knew that a home violently dominated by a strong-minded woman has a way of turning the girls into dependent shadows and the boys into downright ninnies. She realized that the inevitable growth of a healthy child is a drifting away from the home.

So Mrs. Paxton protected herself by enjoying life quite selfishly in her own way. She did not keep young *with* her children or *for* her children—two hollow and disastrous phrases—she kept young for herself. When her children were tiresome she did not scold them; she told them that they bored her.

One of her sons was remarkably handsome and scholastically an utter dunce. I believe she liked him a little the best of the three; but when he was dull she laughed at him and told him so. She called him "the dumb one" without blame or malice, but always with humor. She could do this, because she thought of her children as persons, not as miraculous pieces of personal property.

A man doesn't have to be very smart to do well in this world. In fact, Harry Paxton, though he never could get into college, has done very well since. And the fact that he is "dumb" is to this day a standing joke between him and his mother.

Mrs. Paxton's children were always treated as though they were grown. As they grew older, their private lives were more and more respected and let alone. They chose their schools; they chose their activities; and so long as their friends did not bore Mrs. Paxton or at least were not personally inflicted on her, they chose their own friends. She herself had always been a musician; but as the children showed no predilections in that direction, no music lessons were ever suggested to them. As children, they scarcely existed to her—except in time of sickness; but as persons she got from them a sort of amazed enjoyment. One of her boys was brilliant; she was enormously impressed, exactly as though he had been someone she had read about in the paper. Once she remarked to a shocked and horrified group of mammas that her own daughter, Prudence, would be pretty if she didn't dress so abominably.

Meanwhile she was protecting herself by having a good time, independently of her children. She did as she had always done. Until her children were old enough to share in her amusements, she let them alone in theirs. So far as their amusements were intrinsically interesting they interested her, but she seldom spoiled their game of "pom-pom-pull-away" by playing it with them. She knew that children are happier by themselves, and if she played with them it was only because she wanted the exercise.

It was a sincerely happy home. The children were not compelled or even urged to love one another; and in consequence they grew up with a strong and rather sentimental mutual liking.

Mrs. Paxton's home was a success, because she had a good time in it herself. The children never considered that it was run entirely for their benefit. It was a place where they could do what they liked; but it was distinctly not a place where they could do what they liked to somebody else. It neither restricted them nor did it prostrate itself abjectly before them. It was a place where their father and mother seemed unforgettably happy over mysteries of their own. Even now they pause and wonder what were those amazing and incomprehensible jokes they could not understand. They were welcome to participate in the conversation, if they could, but it was never tempered into one-syllable platitudes for their minds.

Later, when Prudence came to her mother for worldly advice, Mrs. Paxton gave it—gave it as she would have given it to a friend.

So with her son at college. He never felt that there was someone standing behind him with all-forgiving arms. He was on his own. If he failed he would not be blamed, lectured or wept over; but he was not going to be bolstered through with the help of private tutors. Why not? Simply because tutoring would have meant that his mother would have to give up a new dress which she wanted and didn't intend to give up—a straightforward, just and unsentimental reason.

The home was never dull, because it was never compulsory; one could take it or leave it. It was a place where father and mother were happy. It was never insufficient; it had never promised to be a sort of dowdy, downy bed where everyone could indulge his bad habits, be careless in dress and appearance, nag and snarl—in short, a breeding place for petty vices, weaknesses and insufficiencies. In return for giving up the conventional privileges of the mother, of dominating the children and endowing them with convenient, if erroneous, ideas, Mrs. Paxton claimed the right that she should not be dominated, discomforted or "used" by the children.

It is very easy to call her an "unnatural" mother; but being a "natural, old-fashioned mother" is just about the easiest groove for a woman to slide into. It takes much more imagination to be Mrs. Paxton's kind. Motherhood, as a blind, unreasoning habit, is something we have inherited from our ancestors of the cave. This abandonment to the maternal instinct was universal, so we made it sacred—"Hands Off!" But just as we develop, century by century, we fight against the natural, whether it's the natural (and "sacred"?) instinct to kill what we hate or the temptation to abandon oneself to one's children.

It is a commonplace to say that eminent men come, as a rule, from large families; but this is not due to any inherent virtue of the large family in itself; it is because in a large family the children's minds are much more liable to be left alone; each child is not ineradicably stamped with the particular beliefs, errors, convictions, aversions and bogeys that haunted the mother in the year 1889 or 1901 or 1922 as the case might be. In large families no one child can be in so much direct contact with its parents.

Returning to Mrs. Paxton, I want to set down here what happened to her. The three children grew up and left her as children have a way of doing. She missed them, but it did not end her active life, as her active life had always gone along quite independently of them. She never became the miserable mother of the movies, broken by the separation, thankful for one homecoming a year, existing for and ravenously devouring the four letters a month she receives from her scattered daughters and sons. It is someday proved to all women that they do not own their children. They were never meant to.

And Mrs. Paxton had been wise enough never to pretend she owned her children. She had had enough imagination to see that they were primarily persons; and, except in the aforementioned times of sickness, it was as persons that she first thought of them.

So her life went on as it had gone on before. As she grew older her amusements changed, but she grew old slowly. The strange part of it is that the children think of her as a person, not as a "mother" who has to be written to once a fortnight and who will excuse their most intolerable shortcomings.

"What? You've never met my mother?" they say. "Oh, she's a most amazing, most interesting person. She's perfectly charming. You ought to meet her."

They remember their home as the place where their own interests were unhindered, and where, if they were bores, they were snubbed as bores should be snubbed.

"No," cries the sentimentalist; "give me my old wrinkled mother who never thought of anything but me, who gave me the clothes off her back and grew old doing things for my pleasure. Why, I'm the only thing she was ever interested in."

And that's the fate of the mother we exalt at present—on screen and in sob story. Flatter her, "respect" her—and leave her alone. She never had the imagination to consider her children as persons when they were young, so they are unable to think of her as a person when she is old.

They send her a shawl for Christmas. When she visits them twice a year they take her to the Hippodrome: "Mother wouldn't like these new-fashioned shows." She is not a person; she is "poor" mother. Old at fifty, she eats in her room when there's young company at dinner. She has given her children so much in selfish, unreasoning love that when they go from her she has nothing left except the honorary title "mother" on which to feed her ill-nourished soul.

We have learned at last on the advice of our doctors to leave babies alone. No longer do we tease and talk to and "draw out" the baby all day, and wonder why it is fretful and cross and nervous at the day's end. A mother's love for a child is no longer measured by the number of times it cries for her every night. Perhaps someday we'll leave our children alone, too, and spend our time on ourselves. The home is not so much insufficient as it is oversufficient. It is cloying; it tries too hard. A woman happy with her husband is worth a dozen child worshipers in her influence on the child. And all the energy spent in "molding" the child is not as effective as the imagination to see the child as a "person," because sooner or later a person is what that child is going to be.

—*Ladies' Home Journal*, June 1923

How to Live on $36,000 a Year

"You ought to start saving money," The Young Man With a Future assured me just the other day. "You think it's smart to live up to your income. Someday you'll land in the poorhouse."

I was bored, but I knew he was going to tell me anyhow, so I asked him what I'd better do.

"It's very simple," he answered impatiently; "only you establish a trust fund where you can't get your money if you try."

I had heard this before. It is System Number 999. I tried System Number 1 at the very beginning of my literary career four years ago. A month before I was married I went to a broker and asked his advice about investing some money.

"It's only a thousand," I admitted, "but I feel I ought to begin to save right now."

He considered.

"You don't want Liberty Bonds," he said. "They're too easy to turn into cash. You want a good, sound, conservative investment, but also you want it where you can't get at it every five minutes."

He finally selected a bond for me that paid 7 per cent and wasn't listed on the market. I turned over my thousand dollars, and my career of amassing capital began that day.

On that day, also, it ended.

* * *

My wife and I were married in New York in the spring of 1920, when prices were higher than they had been within the memory of man. In the light of after events it seems fitting that our career should have started at that precise point in time. I had just received a large check from the movies and I felt a little patronizing toward the millionaires riding down Fifth Avenue in their limousines—because my income had a way of doubling every month. This was actually the case. It had done so for several months— I had made only thirty-five dollars the previous August, while here in April I was making three thousand—and it seemed as if it was going to do so forever. At the end of the year it must reach half a million. Of course with such a state of affairs, economy seemed a waste of time. So we went to live at the most expensive hotel in New York, intending to wait there until enough money accumulated for a trip abroad.

To make a long story short, after we had been married for three months I found one day to my horror that I didn't have a dollar in the world, and the weekly hotel bill for two hundred dollars would be due next day.

I remember the mixed feelings with which I issued from the bank on hearing the news.

"What's the matter?" demanded my wife anxiously, as I joined her on the sidewalk. "You look depressed."

"I'm not depressed," I answered cheerfully; "I'm just surprised. We haven't got any money."

"Haven't got any money," she repeated calmly, and we began to walk up the Avenue in a sort of trance. "Well, let's go to the movies," she suggested jovially.

It all seemed so tranquil that I was not a bit cast down. The cashier had not even scowled at me. I had walked in and said to him, "How much money have I got?" And he had looked in a big book and answered, "None."

That was all. There were no harsh words, no blows. And I knew that there was nothing to worry about. I was now a successful author, and when successful authors ran out of money all they had to do was to sign checks. I wasn't poor—they couldn't fool me. Poverty meant being depressed and living in a small remote room and eating at a *rôtisserie* on the corner, while I—why, it was impossible that I should be poor! I was living at the best hotel in New York!

My first step was to try to sell my only possession— my $1,000 bond. It was the first of many times I made the attempt. In all financial crises, I dig it out and with it go hopefully to the bank, supposing that, as it never fails to pay the proper interest, it has at last assumed a tangible value. But as I have never been able to sell it, it has gradually acquired the sacredness of a family heirloom. It is always referred to by my wife as "your bond," and it was once turned in at the Subway offices after I left it by accident on a car seat!

This particular crisis passed next morning when the discovery that publishers sometimes advance royalties sent me hurriedly to mine. So the only lesson I learned from it was that my money usually turns up somewhere in time of need, and that at the worst you can always borrow—a lesson that would make Benjamin Franklin turn over in his grave.

For the first three years of our marriage our income averaged a little more than $20,000 a year. We indulged in such luxuries as a baby and a trip to Europe, and always money seemed to come easier and easier with less and less effort, until we felt that with just a little more margin to come and go on we could begin to save.

We left the Middle West and moved east to a town about fifteen miles from New York, where we rented a house for $300 a month. We hired a nurse for $90 a month; a man and his wife—they acted as butler, chauffeur, yard man, cook, parlor maid and chambermaid— for $160 a month; and a laundress, who came twice a week, for $36 a month. This year of 1923, we told each other, was to be our saving year. We were going to earn $24,000, and live on $18,000, thus giving us a surplus of $6,000 with which to buy safety and security for our old age. We were going to do better at last.

Now as everyone knows, when you want to do better you first buy a book and print your name in the front of it in capital letters. So my wife bought a book, and every bill that came to the house was carefully entered in it, so that we could watch living expenses and cut them away to almost nothing—or at least to $1,500 a month.

We had, however, reckoned without our town. It is one of those little towns springing up on all sides of New York which are built especially for those who have made money suddenly but have never had money before.

My wife and I are, of course, members of this newly rich class. That is to say, five years ago we had no money at all, and what we now do away with would have seemed like inestimable riches to us then. I have at times suspected that we are the only newly rich people in America, that in fact we are the very couple at whom all the articles about the newly rich were aimed.

Now when you say "newly rich" you picture a middle-aged and corpulent man who has a tendency to remove his collar at formal dinners and is in perpetual hot water with his ambitious wife and her titled friends. As a member of the newly rich class, I assure you that this picture is entirely libelous. I myself, for example, am a mild, slightly used young man of twenty-seven, and what corpulence I may have developed is for the present a strictly confidential matter between my tailor and me. We once dined with a bona fide nobleman, but we were both far too frightened to take off our collars or even to demand corned beef and cabbage. Nevertheless we live in a town especially prepared for keeping money in circulation.

When we came here, a year ago, there were, all together, seven merchants engaged in the purveyance of food—three grocers, three butchers and a fishman. But when the word went around in food-purveying circles that the town was filling up with the recently enriched as fast as houses could be built for them, the rush of butchers, grocers, fishmen and delicatessen men became enormous. Trainloads of them arrived daily with signs and scales in hand to stake out a claim and sprinkle sawdust upon it. It was like the gold rush of '49, or a big bonanza of the '70's. Older and larger cities were denuded of their stores. Inside of a year eighteen food dealers had set up shop in our main street and might be seen any day waiting in their doorways with alluring and deceitful smiles.

Having long been somewhat overcharged by the seven previous food purveyors we all naturally rushed to the new men, who made it known by large numerical signs in their windows that they intended practically to give food away. But once we were snared, the prices began to rise alarmingly, until all of us scurried like frightened mice from one new man to another, seeking only justice, and seeking it in vain.

What had happened, of course, was that there were too many food purveyors for the population. It was absolutely impossible for eighteen of them to subsist on the town and at the same time charge moderate prices. So each was waiting for some of the others to give up and move away; meanwhile the only way the rest of them could carry their loans from the bank was by selling things at two or three times the prices in the city fifteen miles away. And that is how our town became the most expensive one in the world.

Now in magazine articles people always get together and found community stores, but none of us would consider such a step. It would absolutely ruin us with our neighbors, who would suspect that we actually cared about our money. When I suggested one day to a local lady of wealth—whose husband, by the way, is reputed to have made his money by vending illicit liquids—that I start a community store known as "F. Scott Fitzgerald—Fresh Meats," she was horrified. So the idea was abandoned.

But in spite of the groceries, we began the year in high hopes. My first play was to be presented in the autumn, and even if living in the East forced our expenses a little over $1,500 a month, the play would easily make up for the difference. We knew what colossal sums were earned on play royalties, and just to be sure, we asked several playwrights what was the maximum that could be earned on a year's run. I never allowed myself to be rash. I took a sum halfway between the maximum and the minimum, and put that down as what we could fairly count on its earning. I think my figures came to about $100,000.

It was a pleasant year; we always had this delightful event of the play to look forward to. When the play succeeded we could buy a house, and saving money would be so easy that we could do it blindfolded with both hands tied behind our backs.

As if in happy anticipation we had a small windfall in March from an unexpected source—a moving picture—and for almost the first time in our lives we had enough surplus to buy some bonds. Of course we had "my" bond, and every six months I clipped the little coupon and cashed it, but we were so used to it that we never counted it as money. It was simply a warning never to tie up cash where we couldn't get at it in time of need.

No, the thing to buy was Liberty Bonds, and we bought four of them. It was a very exciting business. I descended to a shining and impressive room downstairs, and under the chaperonage of a guard deposited my $4,000 in Liberty Bonds, together with "my" bond, in a little tin box to which I alone had the key.

I left the bank, feeling decidedly solid. I had at last accumulated a capital. I hadn't exactly accumulated it, but there it was anyhow, and if I had died next day it would have yielded my wife $212 a year for life—or for just as long as she cared to live on that amount.

"That," I said to myself with some satisfaction, "is what is called providing for the wife and children. Now all I have to do is to deposit the $100,000 from my play and then we're through with worry forever."

I found that from this time on I had less tendency to worry about current expenses. What if we did spend a few hundred too much now and then? What if our grocery bills did vary mysteriously from $85 to $165 a month, according as to how closely we watched the kitchen? Didn't I have bonds in the bank? Trying to keep under $1,500 a month the way things were going was merely niggardly. We were going to save on a scale that would make such petty economies seem like counting pennies.

The coupons on "my" bond are always sent to an office on lower Broadway. Where Liberty Bond coupons are sent I never had a chance to find out, as I didn't have the pleasure of clipping any. Two of them I was unfortunately compelled to dispose of just one month after I first locked them up. I had begun a new novel, you see, and it occurred to me it would be much better business in the end to keep at the novel and live on the Liberty Bonds while I was writing it. Unfortunately the novel progressed slowly, while the Liberty Bonds went at an alarming rate of speed. The novel was interrupted whenever there was any sound above a whisper in the house, while the Liberty Bonds were never interrupted at all.

And the summer drifted too. It was an exquisite summer and it became a habit with many world-weary New Yorkers to pass their weekends at the Fitzgerald house in the country. Along near the end of a balmy and insidious August I realized with a shock that only three chapters of my novel were done—and in the little tin safety-deposit vault, only "my" bond remained. There it lay—paying storage on itself and a few dollars more. But never mind; in a little while the box would be bursting with savings. I'd have to hire a twin box next door.

But the play was going into rehearsal in two months. To tide over the interval there were two courses open to me—I could sit down and write some short stories or I could continue to work on the novel and borrow the money to live on. Lulled into a sense of security by our sanguine anticipations I decided on the latter course, and my publishers lent me enough to pay our bills until the opening night.

So I went back to my novel, and the months and money melted away; but one morning in October I sat in the cold interior of a New York theatre and heard the cast read through the first act of my play. It was magnificent; my estimate had been too low. I could almost hear the people scrambling for seats, hear the ghostly voices of the movie magnates as they bid against one another for the picture rights. The novel was now laid aside; my days were spent at the theatre and my nights in revising and improving the two or three little weak spots in what was to be the success of the year.

The time approached and life became a breathless affair. The November bills came in, were glanced at, and punched onto a bill file on the bookcase. More important questions were in the air. A disgusted letter arrived from an editor telling me I had written only two short stories during the entire year. But what did that matter? The main thing was that our second comedian got the wrong intonation in his first-act exit line.

The play opened in Atlantic City in November. It was a colossal frost. People left their seats and walked out; people rustled their programs and talked audibly in bored impatient whispers. After the second act I wanted to stop the show and say it was all a mistake but the actors struggled heroically on.

There was a fruitless week of patching and revising, and then we gave up and came home. To my profound astonishment the year, the great year, was almost over. I was $5,000 in debt, and my one idea was to get in touch with a reliable poorhouse where we could hire a room and bath for nothing a week. But one satisfaction nobody could take from us. We had spent $36,000, and purchased for one year the right to be members of the newly rich class. What more can money buy?

The first move, of course, was to get out "my" bond, take it to the bank and offer it for sale. A very nice old man at a shining table was firm as to its value as security, but he promised that if I became overdrawn he would call me up on the phone and give me a chance to make good. No, he never went to lunch with depositors. He considered writers a shiftless class, he said, and assured me that the whole bank was absolutely burglarproof from cellar to roof.

Too discouraged even to put the bond back in the now yawning deposit box, I tucked it gloomily into my pocket and went home. There was no help for it—I must go to work. I had exhausted my resources and there was nothing else to do. In the train I listed all our possessions on which, if it came to that, we could possibly raise money. Here is the list:

1 Oil stove, damaged.
9 Electric lamps, all varieties.
2 Bookcases with books to match.
1 Cigarette humidor, made by a convict.
2 Framed crayon portraits of my wife and me.
1 Medium-priced automobile, 1921 model.
1 Bond, par value $1,000; actual value unknown.

"Let's cut down expenses right away," began my wife when I reached home. "There's a new grocery in town where you pay cash and everything costs only half what it does anywhere else. I can take the car every morning and—"

"Cash!" I began to laugh at this. "Cash!"

The one thing it was impossible for us to do now was to pay cash. It was too late to pay cash. We had no cash to pay. We should rather have gone down on our knees and thanked the butcher and grocer for letting us charge. An enormous economic fact became clear to me at that moment—the rarity of cash, the latitude of choice that cash allows.

"Well," she remarked thoughtfully, "that's too bad. But at least we don't need three servants. We'll get a Japanese to do general housework, and I'll be nurse for awhile until you get us out of danger."

"Let them go?" I demanded incredulously. "But we can't let them go! We'd have to pay them an extra two weeks each. Why, to get them out of the house would cost us $125—in cash! Besides, it's nice to have the butler; if we have an awful smash we can send him up to New York to hold us a place in the bread line."

"Well, then, how can we economize?"

"We can't. We're too poor to economize. Economy is a luxury. We could have economized last summer—but now our only salvation is in extravagance."

"How about a smaller house?"

"Impossible! Moving is the most expensive thing in the world; and besides, I couldn't work during the confusion. No," I went on, "I'll just have to get out of this mess the only way I know how, by making more money. Then when we've got something in the bank we can decide what we'd better do."

Over our garage is a large bare room whither I now retired with pencil, paper and the oil stove, emerging the next afternoon at five o'clock with a 7,000-word story. That was something; it would pay the rent and last month's overdue bills. It took twelve hours a day for five weeks to rise from abject poverty back into the middle class, but within that time we had paid our debts, and the cause for immediate worry was over.

But I was far from satisfied with the whole affair. A young man can work at excessive speed with no ill effects, but youth is unfortunately not a permanent condition of life.

I wanted to find out where the $36,000 had gone. Thirty-six thousand is not very wealthy—not yacht-and-Palm-Beach wealthy—but it sounds to me as though it should buy a roomy house full of furniture, a trip to Europe once a year, and a bond or two besides. But our $36,000 had bought nothing at all.

So I dug up my miscellaneous account books, and my wife dug up her complete household record for the year 1923, and we made out the monthly average. Here it is:

HOUSEHOLD EXPENSES

	APPORTIONED PER MONTH
Income tax	$198.00
Food	202.00
Rent	300.00

Coal, wood, ice, gas, light, phone and water	114.50
Servants	295.00
Golf clubs	105.50
Clothes—three people	158.00
Doctor and dentist	42.50
Drugs and cigarettes	32.50
Automobile	25.00
Books	14.50
All other household expenses	112.50
Total	$1,600.00

"Well, that's not bad," we thought when we had got thus far. "Some of the items are pretty high, especially food and servants. But there's about everything accounted for, and it's only a little more than half our income."

Then we worked out the average monthly expenditures that could be included under pleasure.

Hotel bills—this meant spending the night or charging meals in New York	$51.00
Trips—only two, but apportioned per month	43.00
Theatre tickets	55.00
Barber and hairdresser	25.00
Charity and loans	15.00
Taxis	15.00
Gambling—this dark heading covers bridge, craps and football bets	33.00
Restaurant parties	70.00
Entertaining	70.00
Miscellaneous	23.00
Total	$400.00

Some of these items were pretty high. They will seem higher to a Westerner than to a New Yorker. Fifty-five dollars for theatre tickets means between three and five shows a month, depending on the type of show and how long it's been running. Football games are also included in this, as well as ringside seats to the Dempsey-Firpo fight. As for the amount marked "restaurant parties"—$70 would perhaps take three couples to a popular after-theatre cabaret—but it would be a close shave.

We added the items marked "pleasure" to the items marked "household expenses," and obtained a monthly total.

"Fine," I said. "Just $3,000. Now at least we'll know where to cut down, because we know where it goes."

She frowned; then a puzzled, awed expression passed over her face.

"What's the matter?" I demanded. "Isn't it all right? Are some of the items wrong?"

"It isn't the items," she said staggeringly; "it's the total. This only adds up to $2,000 a month."

I was incredulous, but she nodded.

"But listen," I protested; "my bank statements show that we've spent $3,000 a month. You don't mean to say that every month we lose $1,000?"

"This only adds up to $2,000," she protested, "so we must have."

"Give me the pencil."

For an hour I worked over the accounts in silence, but to no avail.

"Why, this is impossible!" I insisted. "People don't lose $12,000 in a year. It's just—it's just missing."

There was a ring at the doorbell and I walked over to answer it, still dazed by these figures. It was the Bank-lands, our neighbors from over the way.

"Good heavens!" I announced. "We've just lost $12,000!"

Bankland stepped back alertly.

"Burglars?" he inquired.

"Ghosts," answered my wife.

Mrs. Bankland looked nervously around.

"Really?"

We explained the situation, the mysterious third of our income that had vanished into thin air.

"Well, what we do," said Mrs. Bankland, "is, we have a budget."

"We have a budget," agreed Bankland, "and we stick absolutely to it. If the skies fall we don't go over any item of that budget. That's the only way to live sensibly and save money."

"That's what we ought to do," I agreed.

Mrs. Bankland nodded enthusiastically.

"It's a wonderful scheme," she went on. "We make a certain deposit every month, and all I save on it I can have for myself to do anything I want with."

I could see that my own wife was visibly excited.

"That's what I want to do," she broke out suddenly. "Have a budget. Everybody does it that has any sense."

"I pity anyone that doesn't use that system," said Bankland solemnly. "Think of the inducement to economy— the extra money my wife'll have for clothes."

"How much have you saved so far?" my wife inquired eagerly of Mrs. Bankland.

"So far?" repeated Mrs. Bankland. "Oh, I haven't had a chance so far. You see we only began the system yesterday."

"Yesterday!" we cried.

"Just yesterday," agreed Bankland darkly. "But I wish to heaven I'd started it a year ago. I've been working over our accounts all week, and do you know, Fitzgerald, every month there's $2,000 I can't account for to save my soul."

* * *

Our financial troubles are now over. We have permanently left the newly rich class and installed the budget system. It is simple and sensible, and I can explain it to you in a few words. You consider your income as an enormous pie all cut up into slices, each slice representing one class of expenses. Somebody has worked it all out; so you know just what proportion of your income you can spend on each slice. There is even a slice for founding universities, if you go in for that.

For instance, the amount you spend on the theatre should be half your drug-store bill. This will enable us to see one play every five and a half months, or two and a half plays a year. We have already picked out the first one, but if it isn't running five and a half months from now we shall be that much ahead. Our allowance for newspapers should be only a quarter of what we spend on self-improvement, so we are considering whether to get the Sunday paper once a month or to subscribe for an almanac.

According to the budget we will be allowed only three-quarters of a servant, so we are on the lookout for a one-legged cook who can come six days a week. And apparently the author of the budget book lives in a town where you can still go to the movies for a nickel and get a shave for a dime. But we are going to give up the expenditure called "Foreign missions, etc.," and apply it to the life of crime instead. Altogether, outside of the fact that there is no slice allowed for "missing" it seems to be a very complete book, and according to the testimonials in the back, if we make $36,000 again this year, the chances are that we'll save at least $35,000.

"But we can't get any of that first $36,000 back," I complained around the house. "If we just had something to show for it I wouldn't feel so absurd."

My wife thought a long while.

"The only thing you can do," she said finally, "is to write a magazine article and call it 'How to Live on $36,000 a Year.'"

"What a silly suggestion!" I replied coldly.

—*Saturday Evening Post,* **April 5, 1924**

How to Live on
Practically Nothing a Year

I

"All right," I said hopefully, "what did it come to for the month?"

"Two thousand three hundred and twenty dollars and eighty-two cents."

It was the fifth of five long months during which we had tried by every device we knew of to bring the figure of our expenditures safely below the figure of our income. We had succeeded in buying less clothes, less food and fewer luxuries—in fact, we had succeeded in everything except in saving money.

"Let's give up," said my wife gloomily. "Look—here's another bill I haven't even opened."

"It isn't a bill—it's got a French stamp."

It was a letter. I read it aloud and when I finished we looked at each other in a wild expectant way.

"I don't see why everybody doesn't come over here," it said. "I am now writing from a little inn in France where I just had a meal fit for a king, washed down with champagne, for the absurd sum of sixty-one cents. It costs about one-tenth as much to live over here. From where I sit I can see the smoky peaks of the Alps rising behind a town that was old before Alexander the Great was born—"

By the time we had read the letter for the third time we were in our car bound for New York. As we rushed into the steamship office half an hour later, overturning a rolltop desk and bumping an office boy up against the wall, the agent looked up with mild surprise.

"Don't utter a word," he said. "You're the twelfth this morning and I understand. You've just got a letter from a friend in Europe telling you how cheap everything is and you want to sail right away. How many?"

"One child," we told him breathlessly.

"Good!" he exclaimed, spreading out a deck of cards on his flat table. "The suits read that you are going on a long unexpected journey, that you have illness ahead of you and that you will soon meet a number of dark men and women who mean you no good."

As we threw him heavily from the window his voice floated up to us from somewhere between the sixteenth story and the street:

"You sail one week from tomorrow."

II

Now when a family goes abroad to economize, they don't go to the Wembley exhibition or the Olympic games—in fact they don't go to London and Paris at all but hasten to the Riviera, which is the southern coast of France and which is reputed to be the cheapest as well as the most beautiful locality in the world. Moreover we were going to the Riviera *out of season*, which is something like going to Palm Beach for July. When the Riviera season finishes in late spring, all the wealthy British and Americans move up to Deauville and Trouville, and all the gambling houses and fashionable milliners and jewelers and second-story men close up their establishments and follow their quarry north. Immediately prices fall. The native Riverans, who have been living on rice and fish all winter, come out of their caves and buy a bottle of red wine and splash about for a bit in their own blue sea.

For two reformed spendthrifts the Riviera in summer had exactly the right sound. So we put our house in the hands of six real-estate agents and steamed off to France amid the deafening applause of a crowd of friends on the dock—both of whom waved wildly until we were out of sight.

We felt that we had escaped—from extravagance and clamor and from all the wild extremes among which we had dwelt for five hectic years, from the tradesman who laid for us and the nurse who bullied us and the "couple" who kept our house for us and knew us all too well. We were going to the Old World to find a new rhythm for our lives, with a true conviction that we had left our old selves behind forever,—and with a capital of just over seven thousand dollars.

The sun coming through high French windows woke us one week later. Outside we could hear the high clear honk of strange auto-horns and we remembered that we were in Paris. The baby was already sitting up in her cot ringing the bells which summoned the different *fonctionnaires* of the hotel as though she had determined to start the day immediately. It was indeed *her* day, for we were in Paris for no other reason than to get her a nurse.

"*Entrez!*" we shouted together as there was a knock at the door.

A handsome waiter opened it and stepped inside whereupon our child ceased her harmonizing upon the bells and regarded him with marked disfavor.

"Iss a madamoselle who waited out in the street," he remarked.

"Speak French," I said sternly. "We're all French here."

He spoke French for some time.

"All right," I interrupted after a moment. "Now say that again very slowly in English; I didn't quite understand."

"His name's Entrez," remarked the baby helpfully.

"Be that as it may," I flared up, "his French strikes me as very bad."

We discovered finally that an English governess was outside to answer our advertisement in the paper.

"Tell her to come in."

After an interval a tall, languid person in a Rue de la Paix hat strolled into the room and we tried to look as dignified as is possible when sitting up in bed.

"You're Americans?" she said, seating herself with scornful care.

"Yes."

"I understand you want a nurse. Is this the child?"

"Yes, ma'am."

(Here is some high-born lady of the English court, we thought, in temporarily reduced circumstances.)

"I've had a great deal of experience," she said, advancing upon our child and attempting unsuccessfully to take her hand. "I'm practically a trained nurse; I'm a lady born and I never complain."

"Complain of what?" demanded my wife.

The applicant waved her hand vaguely.

"Oh, the food, for example."

"Look here," I asked suspiciously, "before we go any further, let me ask what salary you've been getting."

"For you," she hesitated, "one hundred dollars a month."

"Oh, you wouldn't have to do the cooking too," we assured her; "it's just to take care of one child."

She arose and adjusted her feather boa with fine scorn.

"You'd better get a French nurse," she said, "if you're *that* kind of people. She won't open the windows at night and your baby will never learn the French word for 'tub' but you'll only have to pay her ten dollars a month."

"Good-bye," we said together.

"I'll come for fifty."

"Good-bye," we repeated.

"For forty,—and I'll do the baby's washing."

"We wouldn't take you for your board."

The hotel trembled slightly as she closed the door.

"Where's the lady gone?" asked our child.

"She's hunting Americans," we said. "She looked in the hotel register and thought she saw Chicago written after our names."

We are always witty like that with the baby—she considers us the most amusing couple she has ever known.

After breakfast I went to the Paris branch of our American bank to get money, but I had no sooner entered it than I wished myself at the hotel, or at least that I had gone in by the back way, for I had evidently been recognized and an enormous crowd began to gather outside. The crowd grew and I considered going to the window and making them a speech but I thought that might only increase the disturbance so I looked around intending to ask someone's advice. I recognized no one, however, except one of the bank officials and a Mr. and Mrs. Douglas Fairbanks from America, who were buying francs at a counter in the rear. So I decided not to show myself and, sure enough, by the time I had cashed my check the crowd had given up and melted away.

I think now that we did well to get away from Paris in nine days—which, after all, was only a week more than we had intended. Every morning a new boat-load of Americans poured into the boulevards and every afternoon our room at the hotel was filled with familiar faces until, except that there was no faint taste of wood-alcohol in the refreshments, we might have been in New York. But at last, with six thousand five hundred dollars remaining and with an English nurse whom we engaged for twenty-six dollars a month, we boarded the train for the Riviera, the hot sweet South of France.

When your eyes first fall upon the Mediterranean you know at once why it was here that man first stood erect and stretched out his arms toward the sun. It is a blue sea—or rather it is too blue for that hackneyed phrase which has described every muddy pool from pole to pole. It is the fairy blue of Maxfield Parrish's pictures, blue like blue books, blue oil, blue eyes, and in the shadow of the mountains a green belt of land runs along the coast for a hundred miles and makes a playground for the world. The Riviera! The names of its resorts, Cannes, Nice, Monte Carlo, call up the memory of a hundred kings and princes who have lost their thrones and come here to die, of mysterious rajahs and beys flinging blue diamonds to English dancing girls, of Russian millionaires tossing away fortunes at roulette in the lost caviar days before the war.

From Charles Dickens to Catherine de Medici, from Prince Edward of Wales in the height of his popularity to Oscar Wilde in the depth of his disgrace, the whole world has come here to forget or to rejoice, to hide its face or have its fling, to build white palaces out of the spoils of oppression or to write the books which some-times batter those palaces down. Under striped awnings beside the sea grand dukes and gamblers and diplomats and noble courtesans and Balkan czars smoked their slow cigarettes while 1913 drifted into 1914 without a quiver of the calendar, and the fury gathered in the north that was to sweep three-fourths of them away.

We reached Hyères, the town of our destination, in the blazing noon, aware immediately of the tropic's breath as it oozed out of the massed pines. A cabby with a large egg-shaped carbuncle in the center of his forehead struggled with a uniformed hotel porter for the possession of our grips.

"Je suis a stranger here," I said in flawless French. "Je veux aller to le best hotel dans le town."

The porter pointed to an imposing autobus in the station drive. On the side was painted "Grand Hôtel de Paris et de Rome."

"Which is the best?" I asked.

For answer he picked up our heaviest grip, balanced it a moment in his hand, hit the cabby a crashing blow on the forehead—I immediately understood the gradual growth of the carbuncle—and then pressed us firmly toward the car. I tossed several nickels—or rather francs—upon the prostrate carbuncular man.

"Isn't it hot," remarked the nurse.

"I like it very much indeed," I responded, mopping my forehead and attempting a cool smile. I felt that the moral responsibility was with me—I had picked out Hyères for no more reason than that a friend had once spent a winter there. Besides we hadn't come here to keep cool—we had come here to economize, to live on practically nothing a year.

"Nevertheless, it's hot," said my wife, and a moment later the child shouted "Coat off!" in no uncertain voice.

"He must think we want to see the town," I said when, after driving for a mile along a palm-lined road, we stopped in an ancient, Mexican-looking square. "Hold on!"

This last was in alarm for he was hurriedly disembarking our baggage in front of a dilapidated quick-lunch emporium. On a ragged awning over its door were the words "Grand Hôtel de Paris et de Rome."

"Is this a joke?" I demanded. "Did I tell you to go to the best hotel in town?"

"Here it is," he said.

"No it isn't. This is the worst one. This is the worst hotel I ever saw."

"I am the proprietor," he said.

"I'm sorry, but we've got a baby here"—the nurse obligingly held up the baby—"and we want a more modern hotel, with a bath."

"We have a bath."

"I mean a private bath."

"We will not use while you are here. All the big hotels have shut up themselves for during the summer."

"I don't believe him for a minute," said my wife.

I looked around helplessly. Two scanty, hungry women had come out of the door and were looking voraciously at our baggage. Suddenly I heard the sound of slow hoofs and glancing up I beheld the carbuncular man driving disconsolately up the dusty street.

"What's le best hotel dans le town?" I shouted at him.

"Non, non, non, non!" he cried, waving his reins excitedly. "Jardin Hôtel open!"

As the proprietor of the Grand Hotel of Paris and of Rome dropped my grip and started toward the cabby at a run, I turned to the hungry women accusingly.

"What do you mean by having a bus like this?" I demanded.

I felt very American and superior; I intimated that if the morals of the French people were in this decadent state I regretted that we had ever entered the war.

"Daddy's hot too," remarked the baby irrelevantly.

"I am not hot!"

"Daddy had better stop talking and find us a hotel," remarked the English nurse, "before we all melt away."

It was the work of but an hour to pay off the proprietor of the Hôtel de Paris et de Rome, to add damages for his wounded feelings and to install ourselves in the Hôtel du Jardin, on the edge of town.

"Hyères," says my guidebook, "is the very oldest and warmest of the Riviera winter resorts and is now frequented almost exclusively by the English." But when we arrived there late in May, even the English, except the very oldest and warmest, had moved away. The Hôtel du Jardin bore traces of having been inhabited—the halls were littered with innumerable old copies of the "Illustrated London News"—but now, as we found at dinner, only a superannuated dozen, a slowly decaying dozen, a solemn and dispirited dozen remained.

But we were to be there merely while we searched for a villa, and it had the advantage of being amazingly cheap for a first-class hotel—the rate for four of us, including meals, was one hundred and fifty francs, less than eight dollars a day.

The real-estate agent, an energetic young gentleman with his pants buttoned snugly around his chest, called on us next morning.

"Dozens of villas," he said enthusiastically. "We will take the horse and buggy and go see."

It was a simmering morning, but the streets already swarmed with the faces of Southern France—dark faces, for there is an Arab streak along the Riviera, left from turbulent, forgotten centuries. Once the Moors harried the coast for gain, and later, as they swept up through Spain in mad glory, they threw out frontier towns along the shores as outposts for their conquest of the world. They were not the first people, or the last, that have tried to overrun France—all that remains now for proud Moslem hopes is an occasional Moorish tower and the tragic glint of black Eastern eyes.

"Now this villa rents for thirty dollars a month," said the real-estate agent as we stopped at a small house on the edge of town.

"What's the matter with it?" asked my wife suspiciously.

"Nothing at all. It is superb. It has six rooms and a well."

"A well?"

"A fine well."

"Do you mean it has no bathroom?"

"Not what you would call an actual bathroom."

"Drive on," we said.

It was obvious by noon that there were no villas to be let in Hyères. They were all too hot, too small, too dirty, or too *triste*, an expressive word which implies that the mad marquis still walks through the halls in his shroud.

"Yes, we have no villas today," remarked the agent, smiling.

"That's a very old played-out joke," I said, "and I am too hot to laugh."

Our clothes were hanging on us like wet towels but when I had established our identity by a scar on my left hand we were admitted to the hotel. I decided to ask one of the lingering Englishmen if there was perhaps another quiet town nearby.

Now, asking something of an American or a Frenchman is a definite thing—the only difference is that you can understand the American's reply. But getting an answer from an Englishman is about as complicated as borrowing a match from the Secretary of State. The first one I approached dropped his paper, looked at me in horror and bolted precipitately from the room. This disconcerted me for a moment but luckily my eyes fell on a man whom I had seen being wheeled in to dinner.

"Good morning," I said. "Could you tell me—" He jerked spasmodically, but to my relief, he was unable to leave his seat. "I wonder if you know a town where I could get a villa for the summer."

"Don't know any at all," he said coldly. "And I wouldn't tell *you* if I did."

He didn't exactly pronounce the last sentence but I could read the words as they issued from his eyes.

"I suppose you're a newcomer too," I suggested.

"I've been here every winter for sixteen years."

Pretending to detect an invitation in this, I drew up my chair.

"Then you must know some town," I assured him.

"Cannes, Nice, Monte Carlo."

"But they're too expensive. I want a quiet place to do a lot of work."

"Cannes, Nice, Monte Carlo. All quiet in summer. Don't know any others. Wouldn't tell you if I did. Good day."

Upstairs the nurse was counting the mosquito bites on the baby, all received during the night, and my wife was adding them up in a big book.

"Cannes, Nice, Monte Carlo," I said.

"I'm glad we're going to leave this broiling town," remarked the nurse.

"I think we'd better try Cannes."

"I think so too," said my wife eagerly. "I hear it's very gay—I mean, it's no economy to stay where you can't work, and I don't believe we can get a villa here after all."

"Let's go on the big boat," said the baby suddenly.

"Silence! We've come to the Riviera and we're here to stay."

So we decided to leave the nurse and baby in Hyères and run up to Cannes, which is a more fashionable town in a more northerly situation along the shore. Now when you "run up" to somewhere, you have to have an automobile, so we bought the only new one in town next day. It had the power of six horses—the age of the horses was not stated—and it was so small that we loomed out of it like giants; so small that you could run it under the verandah for the night. It had no lock, no speedometer, no gauge, and its cost, including the parcel-post charge, was seven hundred and fifty dollars. We started for Cannes in it and, except for the warm exhaust when other cars drove over us, we found the trip comparatively cool.

All the celebrities of Europe have spent a season in Cannes—even the Man with the Iron Mask whiled away twelve years on an island off its shore. Its gorgeous villas are built of stone so soft that it is sawed instead of hewed. We looked at four of them next morning. They were small, neat and clean—you could have matched them in any suburb of Los Angeles. They rented at sixty-five dollars a month.

"I like them," said my wife firmly. "Let's rent one. They look awfully easy to run."

"We didn't come abroad to find a house that was easy to run," I objected. "How could I write looking out on a—" I glanced out the window and my eyes met a splendid view of the sea, "—where I'd hear every whisper in the house."

So we moved on to the fourth villa, the wonderful fourth villa, the memory of which still causes me to lie awake and hope that some bright day will find me there. It rose in white marble out of a great hill, like a chateau, like a castle of old. The very taxi-cab that took us there had romance in its front seat.

"Did you notice our driver?" said the agent, leaning toward me. "He used to be a Russian millionaire."

We peered through the glass at him—a thin dispirited man who ordered the gears about with a lordly air.

"The town is full of them," said the agent. "They're glad to get jobs as chauffeurs, butlers or waiters—the women work as *femmes de chambre* in the hotels."

"Why don't they open tea rooms like Americans do?"

"Most of them aren't fit for anything. We're awfully sorry for them, but—" He leaned forward and tapped on the glass. "Would you mind driving a little faster? We haven't got all day!"

"Look," he said when we reached the chateau on the hill. "There's the Grand Duke Michael's villa next door."

"You mean he's the butler there?"

"Oh, no. He's got money. He's gone north for the summer."

When we had entered through scrolled brass gates that creaked massively as gates should for a king, and when the blinds had been drawn we were in a high central hall hung with ancestral portraits of knights in armor and courtiers in satin and brocade. It was like a movie set. Flights of marble stairs rose in solid dignity to form a grand gallery into which light dropped through blue figured glass upon a mosaic floor. It was modern too,—with huge clean beds and a model kitchen and three bathrooms and a solemn, silent study overlooking the sea.

"It belonged to a Russian general," said the agent, "killed in Silesia during the war."

"How much is it?"

"For the summer—one hundred and ten dollars a month."

"Done!" I said. "Fix up the lease right away. My wife will go to Hyères immediately to get the—"

"Just a minute," she said, frowning. "How many servants will it take to run this house?"

"Why, I should say—" the agent glanced at us sharply and hesitated. "About five."

"I should say about eight." She turned to me. "Let's go to Newport and rent the Vanderbilt house instead."

"Remember," said the agent, "you've got the Grand Duke Michael on your left."

"Will he come to see us?" I inquired.

"He would, of course," explained the agent, "only, you see, he's gone away."

We held debate upon the mosaic floor. My theory was that I couldn't work in the little houses and that this would be a real investment because of its romantic inspiration. My wife's theory was that eight servants eat a lot of food and that it simply wouldn't do. We apologized to the agent, shook hands respectfully with the millionaire taxi-driver, and gave him five francs, and in a state of great dejection returned to Hyères.

"Here's the hotel bill," said my wife as we went despondently in to dinner.

"Thank heaven it's only fifty-five dollars."

I opened it. To my amazement, tax after tax had been added beneath the bill—government tax, city tax, a ten per cent tax to re-tip the servants and the special tax for Americans besides—and the fifty-five dollars had swollen to one hundred and twenty-seven.

I looked gloomily at a nameless piece of meat soaked in a lifeless gravy which reclined on my plate.

"I think it's goat's meat," said the nurse, following my eyes. She turned to my wife. "Did you ever taste goat's meat, Mrs. Fitzgerald?"

But Mrs. Fitzgerald had never tasted goat's meat and Mrs. Fitzgerald had fled.

As I wandered dismally about the hotel next day, hoping that our house on Long Island hadn't been rented so that we could go home for the summer, I noticed that the halls were even more deserted than usual. There seemed to be more old copies of the "Illustrated London News" about, and more empty chairs. At dinner we had the goat again. As I looked around the empty dining room I suddenly realized that the last Englishman had taken his cane and his conscience and fled to London. No wonder there was goat—it would have been a miracle had there been anything else but goat. The management was keeping open a two-hundred-room hotel for us alone!

III

Hyères grew warmer and we rested there in a helpless daze. We knew now why Catherine de Medici had chosen it for her favorite resort. A month of it in the summer and she must have returned to Paris with a dozen St. Bartholomew's sizzling in her head. In vain we took trips to Nice, to Antibes, to Ste. Maxime—we were worried now; a fourth of our seven thousand had slipped away. Then one morning just five weeks after we had left New York we got off the train at a little town called St. Raphaël that we had never considered before.

It was a red little town built close to the sea, with gay red-roofed houses and an air of repressed carnival about it, carnival that would venture forth into the streets before night. We knew that we would love to live in it and we asked a citizen the whereabouts of the real-estate agency.

"Ah, for that you had far better ask the King!" he exclaimed.

A principality! A second Monaco! We had not known there were two of them along the French shore.

"And a bank that will cash a letter of credit?"

"For that, too, you must ask the King."

He pointed the way toward the palace down a long shady street, and my wife hurriedly produced a mirror and began powdering her face.

"But our dusty clothes?" I said modestly. "Do you think the King will—"

He considered.

"I'm not sure about clothes," he answered. "But I think—yes, I think the King will attend to that for you too."

I hadn't meant that, but we thanked him and with much inward trepidation proceeded toward the imperial domain. After half an hour, when royal turrets had failed to rise against the sky, I stopped another man.

"Can you tell us the way to the imperial palace?"

"The *what?*"

"We want to get an interview with His Majesty—His Majesty the King."

The word "King" caught his attention. His mouth opened understandingly and he pointed to a sign over our heads:

"W. F. King," I read, "Anglo-American Bank, Real-Estate Agency, Railroad Tickets, Insurance, Tours and Excursions, Circulating Library."

The potentate turned out to be a brisk efficient Englishman of middle age who had gradually acquired St. Raphaël to himself over a period of twenty years.

"We are Americans come to Europe to economize," I told him. "We've combed the Riviera from Nice to Hyères and haven't been able to find a villa. Meanwhile our money is leaking gradually away."

He leaned back and pressed a button and almost immediately a lean, gaunt woman appeared in the door.

"This is Marthe," he said, "your cook."

We could hardly believe our ears.

"Do you mean you have a villa for us?"

"I have already selected one," he said. "My agents saw you getting off the train."

He pressed another button and a second woman stood respectfully beside the first.

"This is Jeanne, your *femme de chambre*. She does the mending, too, and waits on the table. You pay her thirteen dollars a month and you pay Marthe sixteen dollars. Marthe does the marketing, however, and expects to make a little on the side for herself."

"But the villa?"—

"The lease is being made out now. The price is seventy-nine dollars a month and your check is good with me. We move you in tomorrow."

Within an hour we had seen our home, a clean cool villa set in a large garden on a hill above town. It was what we had been looking for all along. There was a summerhouse and a sand pile and two bathrooms and roses for breakfast and a gardener who called me milord. When we had paid the rent, only thirty-five hundred dollars, half our original capital, remained. But we felt that at last we could begin to live on practically nothing a year.

IV

In the late afternoon of September 1st, 1924, a distinguished-looking young man, accompanied by a young lady in a short, bright blue bathing suit, might have been seen lying on a sandy beach in France. Both of them were burned to a deep chocolate brown so that at first they seemed to be of Egyptian origin; but closer inspection showed that their faces had an Aryan cast and that their voices, when they spoke, had a faintly nasal, North American ring. Near them played a small black child with cotton-white hair who from time to time beat a tin spoon upon a pail and shouted, "*Regardez-moi!*" in no uncertain voice.

Out of the casino nearby drifted weird rococo music—a song dealing with the non-possession of a specific yellow fruit in a certain otherwise well-stocked store. Waiters, both Senegalese and European, rushed around among the bathers with many-colored drinks, pausing now and then to chase away the children of the poor, who were dressing and undressing with neither modesty nor self-consciousness, upon the sand.

"Hasn't it been a good summer!" said the young man, lazily. "We've become absolutely French."

"And the French are such an aesthetic people," said the young lady, listening for a moment to the banana music. "They know how to live. Think of all the nice things they have to eat!"

"Delicious things! Heavenly things!" exclaimed the young man, spreading some American deviled ham on some biscuits marked Springfield, Illinois. "But then they've studied the food question for two thousand years."

"And things are so cheap here!" cried the young lady enthusiastically. "Think of perfume! Perfume that would cost fifteen dollars in New York, you can get here for five."

The young man struck a Swedish match and lit an American cigarette.

"The trouble with most Americans in France," he remarked sonorously, "is that they won't lead a real French life. They hang around the big hotels and exchange opinions fresh from the States."

"I know," she agreed. "That's exactly what it said in the 'New York Times' this morning."

The American music ended and the English nurse arose, implying that it was time the child went home to supper. With a sigh, the young man arose too and shook himself violently, scattering a great quantity of sand.

"We've got to stop on the way and get some Arizon-oil gasoline," he said. "That last stuff was awful."

"The check, suh," said a Senegalese waiter with an accent from well below the Mason-Dixon Line. "That'll be ten francs fo' two glasses of beer."

The young man handed him the equivalent of seventy cents in the gold-colored hat-checks of France. Beer was perhaps a little higher than in America, but then he had had the privilege of hearing the historic banana song on a real, or almost real, jazz band. And waiting for him at home was a regular French supper—baked beans from the quaint old Norman town of Akron, Ohio, an omelette fragrant with la Chicago bacon and a cup of English tea.

But perhaps you have already recognized in these two cultured Europeans the same barbaric Americans who had left America just five months before. And perhaps you wonder that the change could have come about so quickly. The secret is that they had entered fully into the life of the Old World. Instead of patronizing "tourist" hotels they had made excursions to quaint little out-of-the-way restaurants, with the real French atmosphere, where supper for two rarely came to more than ten or fifteen dollars. Not for them the glittering capitals—Paris, Brussels, Rome—they were content with short trips to beautiful historic old towns, such as Monte Carlo, where they once left their automobile with a kindly garage man who paid their hotel bill and bought them tickets home.

Yes, our summer had been a complete success. And we had lived on practically nothing—that is, on practically nothing except our original seven thousand dollars. It was all gone!

The trouble is that we had come to the Riviera out of season,—that is, out of one season but in the middle of another. For in summer the people who are "trying to economize" come south and the shrewd French know that this class is the very easiest game of all—as people who are trying to get something for nothing are very liable to be.

Exactly where the money went we don't know—we never do. There were the servants for example; I was very fond of Marthe and Jeanne (and afterwards of their sisters Eugénie and Serpolette, who came in to help) but on my own initiative it would never have occurred to me to insure them all. Yet that was the law. If Jeanne suffocated in her mosquito netting, if Marthe tripped over a bone and broke her thumb I was responsible. I wouldn't have minded so much except that the "little on the side" that Marthe made in doing our marketing amounted, as I figure, to about forty-five per cent.

Our weekly bills at the grocer's and the butcher's averaged sixty-five dollars—or higher than they had ever been in an expensive Long Island town. Whatever the meat actually cost it was almost invariably inedible, while as for the milk every drop of it had to be boiled because the cows were tubercular in France. For fresh vegetables we had tomatoes and a little asparagus, that was all—the only garlic that can be put over on us must be administered in sleep. I wondered often how the Riviera middle class—the bank clerk, say, who supports a family on from forty to seventy dollars a month—manages to keep alive.

"It's even worse in winter," a little French girl told us on the beach. "The English and Americans drive the prices up until we can't buy and we don't know what to do. My sister had to go to Marseilles and find work and she's only fourteen. Next winter I'll go too."

There simply isn't enough to go around—and the Americans who, because of their own high standard of material comfort, want the best obtainable, naturally have to pay. And in addition, the sharp French tradesmen are always ready to take advantage of a careless American eye.

"I don't like this bill," I said to the food-and-ice deliverer. "I arranged to pay you five francs and not eight francs a day."

He became unintelligible for a moment to gain time.

"My wife added it up," he said.

Those valuable Riviera wives! Always they are adding up their husbands' accounts and the dear ladies simply don't know one figure from another. Such a talent in the wife of a railroad president would be an asset worth many million dollars.

It is twilight as I write this and out of my window darkening banks of trees, set one clump behind another in many greens, slope down to the evening sea. The flaming sun has collapsed behind the peaks of the Estérels and the moon already hovers over the Roman aqueducts of Fréjus, five miles away. In half an hour Renée and Bobbé, officers of aviation, are coming to dinner in their white ducks and Renée, who is only twenty-three and has never recovered from having missed the war, will tell us romantically how he wants to smoke opium in Peking and how he writes a few things "for myself alone." Afterwards in the garden their white uniforms will grow dimmer as the more liquid dark comes down, until they, like the heavy roses and the nightingales in the pines, will seem to take an essential and indivisible part in the beauty of this proud gay land.

And though we have saved nothing we have danced the *carmagnole* and, except for the day when my wife took the mosquito lotion for a mouth wash and the time when I tried to smoke a French cigarette and, as Ring Lardner would say, "swooned," we haven't yet been sorry that we came.

The dark-brown child is knocking at the door to bid me good-night.

"Going on the big boat, Daddy?" she says in broken English.

"No."

"Why?"

"Because we're going to try it for another year, and besides—think of perfume!"

We are always like that with the baby. She considers us the wittiest couple she has ever known.

—*Saturday Evening Post*, September 20, 1924

"Wait Till You Have Children of Your Own!"

The original younger generation (I mean, of course, the one that burst forth back in 1919 and got itself thoroughly talked over) used to be periodically squelched with that ominous refrain. Well, the original younger generation are parents now. They are looking at the new world which has established itself out of the confusion of the war, and trying to decide just how their children's education shall differ from their own.

When I say education I mean the whole bag of habits and ideals and prejudices that children receive from their parents between the ages of two and sixteen. I mean more than that—I mean what my own father meant when he said one day that he hoped my life would be different from his. He wanted me to have a better equipment than he had with which to face the world.

All parents want that for their children—except those so smug and self-satisfied that they hope their children will be exactly like themselves. For one parent who sits back at forty now and says to his offspring:

"Look upon this perfect man (or woman) that the Lord made as an example for you"—

There are three who believe the children should be an improvement on their parents, who want their children not to follow blindly in their steps but rather to profit by their mistakes.

Now, ideals, conventions, even truth itself, are continually changing things so that the milk of one generation may be the poison of the next. The young Americans of my time have seen one of these transformations with their own eyes, and for this reason they will not make the initial mistake of trying to teach their children too much. Before a man is thirty he has already accumulated, along with a little wisdom, a great quantity of dust and rubbish in his mind, and the difficulty is to let the children profit by what is wise without unloading the dust and rubbish on them too. We can only try to do better at it than the last generation did—when a generation succeeds in doing it completely, in handing down all its discoveries and none of its delusions, its children shall inherit the earth.

To begin with, my child will have to face conditions of which I am utterly unaware. He may live in a communist state or marry a girl from Mars or sit under an electric fan at the North Pole. Only one thing can I be sure of about the world in which he will live—it will not be as cheerful a world as the world into which I was born. Never had faith in the destiny of man reached such a height as during the nineties—seldom has it ebbed so low as it has now. When we see around us a great decay in ideals of conduct there is some fundamental cause behind it. It is impossible to be vicious in a vacuum. Something serious (which only professional evangelists, cheap novelists, and corrupt politicians profess to understand) is the matter with the world. It will be a strong heart that can fight its way upstream in these troubled waters and not be, like my generation, a bit cynical, a bit weary, and a bit sad. We have seen the war and its attendant ferocity, the hysteria both of the communists and, over here, of the "100%

Americans," the cheating of the wounded veterans, the administration corruption, the prohibition scandal—what wonder if we are almost afraid to open the newspapers in the morning lest our eyes fall on some new rift in civilization, some new vileness in the dark chamber which we call the human heart!

On such a world our children are now opening their eyes. Not long ago I was in a room where lay a young mother whose first child had just been born. She was a young woman of exceptional culture and education who had always had the good things of this world and who can expect to have them until she dies. When she awakened from the ether she turned to the nurse with a question, and bending over her the nurse whispered:

"You have a beautiful little girl."

"A girl?" The young mother's eyes opened and then closed again. Suddenly she began to cry.

"All right," she said brokenly, "I'm glad it's a girl. And I hope she'll be a fool—that's the best thing a girl can be in this world, a beautiful little fool!"

Of course, despite everything, few of us are sick enough, or perhaps logical enough, for such pessimism. We do not want our daughters to be beautiful little fools or our sons to be mere "healthy animals," despite the suffering that it might save them. More than that, we want them to have ideas above the bank book and the comfortable house. We want them to be decent, honorable, and, if I can no longer conscientiously add law-abiding, at least capable of voting against laws which they cannot obey.

I can imagine a young father born as I was in the middle nineties talking somewhat like this to his brand-new son:

"I don't want you to be like me," he says, standing over the baby's bed. "I want you to have time for the finer things in life. I want you to go into politics where not one man in ten has clean hands, and keep your hands clean. Or if you're a business man I want you to be a better kind of business man than I am. Why, my son, except for a few detective stories, I haven't read a book since I left college. My idea of amusement is to play golf or bridge with a lot of people just as dumb as I am, with a bottle of bootleg gin on the side so we won't know how dull we are. I don't know anything about science, or literature, or art, or architecture, or even economics. I believe everything I read in the papers, just like my janitor does. Except for my business I'm almost a half-wit, scarcely fit to vote— but I want you to be something better, and I'm going to give you a chance, so help me God."

Now, that isn't at all what his own father said to *him* way back in 1896. The older man probably talked something like this:

"I want you to be a success. I want you to work hard and make a lot of money. Don't let anybody cheat you, and don't cheat anybody else, or you'll get put in jail. Remember, you're an American"—(here substitute Englishman, Frenchman, or German, for the same speech was being made in many languages)—"and we're much better than any other race, so just remember that everything we don't believe right here in this nation is pretty sure to be wrong. I went to college and I read the papers, so I ought to know."

You recognize this? It is the philosophy of the nineteenth century, the philosophy of personal selfishness and national conceit that led to the Great War and was indirectly responsible for the bloody deaths of many million young men.

At any rate, the new baby, our baby, starts out with something a little different. Having been in the war, and perhaps seen actual fighting, his father doesn't hate the

Germans—he leaves that to the non-combatants—and maybe he remembers that life in Paris can be just as pleasant as life in Podunk, Indiana. He doesn't give a whoop whether his son sings the national anthem in school, because he knows that surface patriotism means less than nothing, and that Grover Cleveland Bergdoll's childish treble once piped out "My Country, 'Tis of Thee" at Teacher's command. This young father hasn't any unnatural faith in the schools anyhow—good as they are—because he knows the teachers are people just like him, not geniuses, but simply hard-working, half-educated young men and women who earn their bread by doing the best they can. He knows that the schools are of necessity a stereotyping agency in a somewhat stereotyped country. What the child will learn are the ideals of a busy shopkeeper, with side glances at the pictures of Abraham Lincoln and George Washington on the wall—those two romantic Presidents who are fast being made into illustrations for Sunday-school books by silly biographers and sloppy short-story writers.

No, the young father knows that his children are not likely to find ideals in school with which to face the modern world. If the child's soul is going to bear any imprint except a few outworn rubber stamps, he must get his inspiration at home. A school system is such a colossal undertaking that it must often be regulated by convenience. But the young father does not have to tell his children shoddy lies about life because of convenience. And I don't believe he will—the bitterest critics of this generation cannot accuse it of mock modesty. Its children will have at least that advantage over my contemporaries, who learned all the filthy words in the English language before they knew anything of the side of life they so grossly misrepresented.

Now I don't mean to give the impression that the

young men and women of my generation are bulging with a hundred sure-fire ways of turning children into veritable Abraham Lincolns. On the contrary, they will be inclined to protect their children from the canned rubbish at large in the world. They know that the knowledge of one good book, Van Loon's "Story of Mankind" for example, is worth a list of a hundred "Children's Classics" compiled by some senile professor. And as they dread canned culture for their child so, more than against anything else, will they protect him from the canned inspiration that has become a national nuisance. The friendship of one older man of wisdom and character is a great boon—but such men are rare, there are not three to every city. And the substitute, the lectures by professional educationalists and boy-thrillers, represents, I think, a very real danger.

It is the danger of overstimulation. A boy or a girl that comes home every day from school with a new idea about beautifying the home or collecting old clothes for the Laplanders or making one noble sacrifice every week, is not a boy or girl whose brain will be anything but a cluttered bird's nest in a few years. I do not want my child's mind stimulated by every quack in the world, from paid patriots to moving-picture magnates who have rummaged among the ash heaps for shoddy ideas to give to the young. Eventually, of course, the child will grow tired both of the radio and of uplifting the neighbors, and there is no individual means of diversion to which I object—but the continual round of them dulls a child's enthusiasm and permanently injures his mind. He is unable to enjoy or even to understand everything that is not presented to him in canned, predigested form—canned music, canned inspiration, even canned play—until it is no wonder that when he is a man he will be ripe for canned opinions and canned ideals.

"But," objects the realist, "your children will grow up

like mine into a world over which you have no control. If you forbid him all these things, will you not be setting up a ring of prohibitions around him—just as a short while since you objected to having about you?"

I'm going to try and answer that question, but first I want to discuss one important respect in which my child's attitude toward life will be different from my own.

It is simply this: whatever respect he may hold for the opinions of age will be taken from him. Unless my mind fails and I join the common conspiracy to teach children that their parents are better than they are, I shall teach my child to respect nothing because it is old, but only those things which he considers worthy of respect. I shall tell him that I know very little more than he knows about the purpose of life in this world, and I shall send him to school with the warning that the teacher is just as ignorant as I am. This is because *I want my children to feel alone*. I want them to take life seriously from the beginning with neither dependency nor a sense of humor, and I want them to know the truth—that they are lost in a strange world compared to which the mystery of all the caves and forests is as nothing. The Russian Jewish newsboy on the streets of New York has an enormous commercial advantage over our children, because he feels alone. He is aware of the vastness and mercilessness of life, and he gets his own knowledge of humanity for himself. Each time he falls down he is not picked up and set on his feet.

I cannot give my son that advantage without exposing him to the thousand dangers of a vagabond's life—but I can make him feel mentally alone, as every great man has been in his heart—alone in his convictions which he forms for himself, and in his character which expresses those convictions. Not only will I force no standards on my son but I will question what others tell him about life. A supreme confidence is one of a man's greatest assets, and we know from the story of our great men that it comes only through self-reliance—and nothing that can be told my son will be of any value to him beside what he finds out for himself. All I can do is watch the vultures who swarm outside with conventional lies for his ear. The best friend we ever have in our adolescence is the one who teaches us to question and to doubt—I would be that kind of friend to my son.

Here, then, are five ways in which my child's early world will be different from my own:

First—He will be less provincial, less patriotic. He will be taught that a citizen of the world is of more value to Podunk, Indiana, than is a citizen of Podunk, Indiana, to Podunk, Indiana. He will be taught to look closely at American ideals, to laugh at those that are absurd, to scorn those that are narrow and small, and give his best to those few in which he believes.

Second—He will know everything about his body from his head to his feet before he is ten years old. It is better that he should know this than that he should learn to read and write.

Third—He will be put as little as possible in the way of constant stimulation whether by men or by machines. Any enthusiasm he has will be questioned, and if it is mob enthusiasm—he who lynches negroes and he who weeps over Pollyanna is equally low at heart—it will be laughed out of him as something unworthy.

Fourth—He shall not respect age unless it is worthy in itself, but he shall look with suspicion on all that his elders say. If he does not agree with them he shall hold his own opinions rather than theirs, not only because he may prove to be right but because he must find out for himself that fire burns.

Fifth—He shall take life seriously and feel always alone: that no one is guiding him, no one directing him, and that he must form his own convictions and standards in a world where no one knows much more than another.

He'll have then, I hope with all my heart, these five things—a citizenship in the world, a knowledge of the body in which he is to live, a hatred of sham, a suspicion of authority, and a lonely heart. Their five opposites— patriotism, modesty, general enthusiasm, faith, and good-fellowship—I leave to the pious office boys of the last generation. They are not for our children.

That much I can do—further than that it depends on the capabilities of the boy—on his intelligence and his inherent honor. Let us suppose that, having these things, he came to me at fourteen and said:

"Father, show me a good great man."

I would have to look around in the living world and find someone worthy of his admiration.

Now no generation in the history of America has ever been so dull, so worthless, so devoid of ideas as that generation which is now between forty and sixty years old— the men who were young in the nineties. I do not, of course, refer to the exceptional people in that generation, but to the general run of "educated" men. They are, as a rule, ill-read, intolerant, pathetic in their mental and spiritual poverty, sharp in business, and bored at home. Culturally they are not only below their own fathers who were fed on Huxley, Spencer, Newman, Carlyle, Emerson, Darwin, and Lamb, but they are also below their much-abused sons who read Freud, Remy de Gourmont, Shaw, Bertrand Russell, Nietzsche, and Anatole France. They were brought up on Anthony Hope and are slowly growing senile on J. S. Fletcher's detective stories and "Foster's Bridge." They claim that such things "relax their minds," which means that they are too illiterate to enjoy anything else. To hear them talk, of course, you would think that they had each individually invented the wireless telegraph, the moving picture, and the telephone—in point of fact, they are almost barbarians.

Whom could my generation look up to in such a crowd? Whom, in fact, could we look up to at all when we were young? My own heroes were men my own age or a little older—men like Ted Coy, the Yale football star. I admired Richard Harding Davis in default of someone better, a certain obscure Jesuit priest, and, occasionally, Theodore Roosevelt. In Taft, McKinley, Bryan, Generals Miles and Shafter, Admirals Schley and Dewey, William Dean Howells, Remington, Carnegie, James J. Hill, Rockefeller, and John Drew, the popular figures of twenty years ago, a little boy could find little that was inspiring. There are good men in this list—notably Dewey and Hill, but they are not men to whom a little boy's heart can go out, not men like Stonewall Jackson, Father Damien, George Rogers Clark, Major André, Byron, Jeb Stuart, Garibaldi, Dickens, Roger Williams, or General Gordon. They were not men half as good as these. Not one of them sounded any high note of heroism, no clear and distinct call to something above and beyond life. Later, when I was grown, I learned to admire a few other Americans of that generation—Stanford White, E. H. Harriman, and Stephen Crane. Here were figures more romantic, men of great dreams, of high faith in their work, who looked beyond the petty ideals of the American nineties—Harriman with his transcontinental railroad, and White with his vision of a new architectural America. But in my lifetime these three men, whose free spirits were incapable of hypocrisy, moved under a cloud.

Now, ten years from today, I hope that if my son comes to me and says, "Father, show me a good man," I can point out something better for him to admire than shrewd politicians or paragons of thrift. Some of those who went to prison for their consciences' sake in 1917 are of my generation, and some who left legs and arms in France and came back to curse not the Germans but the "dollar-a-year men" who fought the war from easy chairs. There have been writers already in my time who have lifted up their voices fearlessly in scorn of sham and hypocrisy and corruption—Cummings, Otto Braun, Dos Passos, Wilson, Ferguson, Thomas Boyd. And in politics there have been young men like Cleveland and Bruce at Princeton, whose names were in the papers before they were twenty because they scrutinized rather than accepted blindly the institutions under which they lived. Oh, we shall have something to show our sons, I think—to point at and say—not, perhaps, "There is a perfect man," but "There is a man who has tried, who has faced life thinking that it could be fuller and freer than it is now and hoping that in some way he could help to make it so."

The women of my generation present a somewhat different problem—I mean the young women who were lately flappers and now have babies at their breasts. Personally I can no more imagine having fallen in love with an old-fashioned girl than with an Amazon—but I think that on the whole the young women of the well-to-do middle classes are somewhat below the men. I refer to the dependent woman, the ex-society girl. She was pretty busy in her adolescence, far too busy to take an education, and what she knows she has learned vicariously from a chance clever man or two that have come her way. Of a far better type are the working girls of the middle classes, the thousands of young women who are the power behind some stupid man in a thousand offices all over the United States. I don't mean that she will bear a race of heroes simply because she has struggled herself—on the contrary, she will probably overemphasize to the children the value of conformity and industry and commercial success—but she is a far higher type of woman than our colleges or our country clubs produce. Women learn best not from books or from their own dreams but from reality and from contact with first-class men. A man can live with a fool all his life untouched by her stupidity, but a smart woman married to a stupid man acquires eventually the man's stupidity and, what is worse, the man's narrow outlook on life.

And this brings on a statement with which many people will disagree violently, a statement which will seem reactionary and out of place here. I hope for the newest generation that it will not be so women-educated as the last. Our fathers were too busy to know much about us until we were fairly well grown, and in consequence such a condition came about that, as Booth Tarkington justly remarked, "All American children belonged to their mother's families." When I said the other day before some members of the Lucy Stone League that most American boys learned to lie at some lady teacher's knee, a shocked silence fell. Nevertheless I believe it to be true. It is not good for boys to be reared altogether by women as American children are. There is something inherent in the male mind that will lie to or impose upon a woman as it would never consider doing to a man.

"If the boys at school don't like you, come here to me," says the mother to her sons.

"If the boys at school don't like you, I want to know the reason why," says the father.

Properly the young boy needs to meet both these two attitudes at home, but my generation got only the first, and it made us soft; and we would still be soft, unpleasantly soft, if we had not had the two years' discipline of the war.

And so, if the young men whom I see every day are typical of their generation, we have by no means hauled down our flags and moderated our opinions and decided to bring up our children in the "good old way." The "good old way" is not nearly good enough for us. That we shall use every discovery of science in the preservation of our children's health goes without saying; but we shall do more than this—we shall give them a free start, not loading them up with our own ideas and experiences, nor advising them to live according to our lights. We were burned in the fire here and there, but—who knows?— fire may not burn our children, and if we warn them away from it they may end by never growing warm. We will not even inflict our cynicism on them as the sentimentality of our fathers was inflicted on us. The most we will urge is a little doubt, asking that the doubt be exercised on our ideas as well as on all the mortal things in this world. Already they are on their heath, charming us with strange new promises in their eyes as they open them upon the world, with their freshness and beauty and the healthy quiet with which they sleep. We shall not ask much of them—love if it comes freely, a little politeness, that is all. They are free, they are little people already, and who are we to stand in their light? They must fight us down at the end, as each generation fights down the one before, the one that is cluttering up the earth with all those decayed notions which it calls its ideals. And if my child is a better man than I, he will come to me at the last and say, not "Father, you were right about life," but "Father, you were entirely wrong."

And when that time comes, as come it will, may I have the justice and the sense to say: "Good luck to you and good-bye, for I owned this world of yours once, but I own it no longer. Go your way now strenuously into the fight, and leave me in peace, among all the warm wrong things that I have loved, for I am old, and my work is done."

—*Woman's Home Companion*, July 1924

How to Waste Material—
A Note on My Generation

I

Ever since Irving's preoccupation with the necessity for an American background, for some square miles of cleared territory on which colorful varia might presently arise, the question of material has hampered the American writer. For one Dreiser who made a single-minded and irreproachable choice there have been a dozen like Henry James who have stupid-got with worry over the matter, and yet another dozen who, blinded by the fading tail of Walt Whitman's comet, have botched their books by the insincere compulsion to write "significantly" about America.

Insincere because it is not a compulsion found in themselves—it is "literary" in the most belittling sense. During the past seven years we have had at least half a dozen treatments of the American farmer, ranging from New England to Nebraska; at least a dozen canny books about youth, some of them with surveys of the American universities for background; more than a dozen novels reflecting various aspects of New York, Chicago, Washington, Detroit, Indianapolis, Wilmington and Richmond; innumerable novels dealing with American politics, business, society, science, racial problems, art, literature and moving pictures, and with Americans abroad at peace or in war; finally several novels of change and growth, tracing the swift decades for their own sweet lavender or protesting vaguely and ineffectually against the industrialization of our beautiful old American life. We have had an Arnold Bennett for every five towns—surely by this time the foundations have been laid! Are we competent only to toil forever upon a never completed first floor whose specifications change from year to year?

In any case we are running through our material like spendthrifts—just as we have done before. In the nineties there began a feverish search for any period of American history that hadn't been "used," and once found it was immediately debauched into a pretty and romantic story. These past seven years have seen the same sort of literary gold rush and for all our boasted sincerity and sophistication, the material is being turned out raw and undigested in much the same way. One author goes to a midland farm for three months to obtain the material for an epic of the American husbandman! Another sets off on a like errand to the Blue Ridge Mountains, a third departs with a Corona for the West Indies—one is justified in the belief that what they get hold of will weigh no more than the journalistic loot brought back by Richard Harding Davis and John Fox, Jr., twenty years ago.

Worse, the result will be doctored up to give it a literary flavor. The farm story will be sprayed with a faint dilution of ideas and sensory impressions from Thomas Hardy; the novel of the Jewish tenement block will be festooned with wreaths from "Ulysses" and the later Gertrude Stein; the document of dreamy youth will be prevented from fluttering entirely away by means of great and half-great names—Marx, Spencer, Wells, Edward Fitzgerald—dropped like paper-weights here and there upon the pages. Finally the novel of business will be cudgeled into being satire by the questionable but constantly reiterated implication that the author and his readers don't partake of the American commercial instinct.

And most of it—the literary beginnings of what was to have been a golden age—is as dead as if it had never been written. Scarcely one of those who put so much effort and enthusiasm, even intelligence, into it, got hold of any material at all.

To a limited extent this was the fault of two men—one of whom, H. L. Mencken, has yet done more for American letters than any man alive. What Mencken felt the absence of, what he wanted, and justly, back in 1920, got away from him, got twisted in his hand. Not because the "literary revolution" went beyond him but because his idea had always been ethical rather than aesthetic. In the history of culture no pure aesthetic idea has ever served as an offensive weapon. Mencken's invective, sharp as Swift's, made its point by the use of the most forceful prose style now written in English. Immediately, instead of committing himself to an infinite series of pronouncements upon the American novel, he should have modulated his tone to the more urbane, more critical one of his early essay on Dreiser.

But perhaps it was already too late. Already he had begotten a family of hammer and tongs men—insensitive, suspicious of glamour, preoccupied exclusively with the external, the contemptible, the "national" and the drab, whose style was a debasement of his least effective manner and who, glib children, played continually with his themes in his maternal shadow. These were the men who manufactured enthusiasm when each new mass of raw data was dumped on the literary platform—mistaking incoherence for vitality, chaos for vitality. It was the "new poetry movement" over again, only that this time its victims were worth the saving. Every week some new novel gave its author membership in "that little band who are producing a worthy American literature." As one of the charter members of that little band I am proud to state that it has now swollen to seventy or eighty members.

And through a curious misconception of his work, Sherwood Anderson must take part of the blame for this enthusiastic march up a blind alley in the dark. To this day reviewers solemnly speak of him as an inarticulate, fumbling man, bursting with ideas—when, on the contrary, he is the possessor of a brilliant and almost inimitable prose style, and of scarcely any ideas at all. Just as the prose of Joyce in the hands of, say, Waldo Frank becomes as insignificant and idiotic as the automatic writing of a Kansas Theosophist, so the Anderson admirers set up Hergesheimer as an antichrist and then proceed to imitate Anderson's lapses from that difficult simplicity they are unable to understand. And here again critics support them by discovering merits in the very disorganization that is to bring their books to a timely and unregretted doom.

Now the business is over. "Wolf" has been cried too often. The public, weary of being fooled, has gone back to its Englishmen, its memoirs and its prophets. Some of the late brilliant boys are on lecture tours (a circular informs me that most of them are to speak upon "the literary revolution"!), some are writing pot-boilers, a few have definitely abandoned the literary life—they were never sufficiently aware that material, however closely observed, is as elusive as the moment in which it has its existence unless it is purified by an incorruptible style and by the catharsis of a passionate emotion.

Of all the work by the young men who have sprung up since 1920 one book survives—"The Enormous Room" by E. E. Cummings. It is scarcely a novel; it doesn't deal with the American scene; it was swamped in the mediocre downpour, isolated—forgotten. But it lives on, because those few who cause books to live have not been able to endure the thought of its mortality. Two other books, both about the war, complete the possible salvage from the work of the younger generation—"Through the Wheat" and "Three Soldiers," but the former despite its fine last chapters doesn't stand up as well as "Les Croix de Bois" and "The Red Badge of Courage," while the latter is marred by its pervasive flavor of contemporary indignation. But as an augury that someone has profited by this dismal record of high hope and stale failure comes the first work of Ernest Hemingway.

II

"In Our Time" consists of fourteen stories, short and long, with fifteen vivid miniatures interpolated between them. When I try to think of any contemporary American short stories as good as "Big Two-Hearted River," the last one in the book, only Gertrude Stein's "Melanctha," Anderson's "The Egg," and Lardner's "Golden Honeymoon" come to mind. It is the account of a boy on a fishing trip— he hikes, pitches his tent, cooks dinner, sleeps and next morning casts for trout. Nothing more—but I read it with the most breathless unwilling interest I have experienced since Conrad first bent my reluctant eyes upon the sea.

The hero, Nick, runs through nearly all the stories, until the book takes on almost an autobiographical tint— in fact "My Old Man," one of the two in which this element seems entirely absent, is the least successful of all. Some of the stories show influences but they are invariably absorbed and transmuted, while in "My Old Man" there is an echo of Anderson's way of thinking in those sentimental "horse stories," which inaugurated his respectability and also his decline four years ago.

But with "The Doctor and the Doctor's Wife," "The End of Something," "The Three Day Blow," "Mr. and Mrs. Elliot" and "Soldier's Home" you are immediately aware of something temperamentally new. In the first of these a man is backed down by a half-breed Indian after committing himself to a fight. The quality of humiliation in the story is so intense that it immediately calls up every such incident in the reader's past. Without a comment or a pointing finger one knows exactly the sharp emotion of young Nick who watches the scene.

The next two stories describe an experience at the last edge of adolescence. You are constantly aware of the continual snapping of ties that is going on around Nick. In the half-stewed, immature conversation before the fire you watch the awakening of that vast unrest that descends upon the emotional type at about eighteen. Again there is not a single recourse to exposition. As in "Big Two-Hearted River," a picture—sharp, nostalgic, tense—develops before your eyes. When the picture is complete a light seems to snap out, the story is over. There is no tail, no sudden change of pace at the end to throw into relief what has gone before.

Nick leaves home penniless; you have a glimpse of him lying wounded in the street of a battered Italian town, and later of a love affair with a nurse on a hospital roof in Milan. Then in one of the best of the stories he is home again. The last glimpse of him is when his mother asks him, with all the bitter world in his heart, to kneel down beside her in the dining room in Puritan prayer.

Anyone who first looks through the short interpolated sketches will hardly fail to read the stories themselves. "The Garden at Mons" and "The Barricade" are profound essays upon the English officer, written on a postage stamp. "The King of Greece's Tea Party," "The Shooting of the Cabinet Ministers" and "The Cigar-store Robbery" particularly fascinated me, as they did when Edmund Wilson first showed them to me in an earlier pamphlet, over two years ago.

Disregard the rather ill-considered blurbs upon the cover. It is sufficient that here is no raw food served up by the railroad restaurants of California and Wisconsin. In the best of these dishes there is not a bit to spare. And many of us who have grown weary of admonitions to "watch this man or that" have felt a sort of renewal of excitement at these stories wherein Ernest Hemingway turns a corner into the street.

—*The Bookman,* May 1926

Princeton

In preparatory school and up to the middle of sophomore year in college, it worried me that I wasn't going
and hadn't gone to Yale. Was I missing a great American secret? There was a gloss upon Yale that Princeton
lacked; Princeton's flannels hadn't been pressed for a
week, its hair always blew a little in the wind. Nothing
was ever carried through at Princeton with the same per-
fection as the Yale Junior Prom or the elections to their
senior societies. From the ragged squabble of club elections with its scars of snobbishness and adolescent heart-
break, to the enigma that faced you at the end of senior
year as to what Princeton *was* and what, bunk and cant
aside, it really stood for, it never presented itself with
Yale's hard, neat, fascinating brightness. Only when you
tried to tear part of your past out of your heart, as I once
did, were you aware of its power of arousing a deep and
imperishable love.

Princeton men take Princeton for granted and resent
any attempt at analysis. As early as 1899 Jesse Lynch
Williams was anathematized for reporting that Princeton
wine helped to make the minutes golden. If the Princetonian had wanted to assert in sturdy chorus that his college was the true flower of American democracy, was
deliberately and passionately America's norm in ideals of
conduct and success, he would have gone to Yale. His
brother and many of the men from his school went there.

Contrariwise he chooses Princeton because at seventeen the furies that whip on American youth have become too coercive for his taste. He wants something quieter, mellower and less exigent. He sees himself being caught up into a wild competition that will lead him headlong into New Haven and dump him pell-mell out into the world. The series of badges which reward the winner of each sprint are no doubt desirable, but he seeks the taste of pleasant pastures and a moment to breathe deep and ruminate before he goes into the clamorous struggle of American life. He finds at Princeton other men like himself and thus is begotten Princeton's scoffing and mildly ironic attitude toward Yale.

Harvard has never existed as a conception at Princeton. Harvard men were "Bostonians with affected accents," or they were "That Isaacs fellow who got the high school scholarship out home." Lee Higginson & Company hired their athletes for them but no matter how much one did for Harvard one couldn't belong to "Fly" or "Porcellian" without going to Groton or St. Mark's. Such ideas were satisfying if inaccurate, for Cambridge, in more senses than one, was many miles away. Harvard was a series of sporadic relationships, sometimes pleasant, sometimes hostile—that was all.

Princeton is in the flat midlands of New Jersey, rising, a green Phoenix, out of the ugliest country in the world. Sordid Trenton sweats and festers a few miles south; northward are Elizabeth and the Erie Railroad and the suburban slums of New York; westward the dreary upper purlieus of the Delaware River. But around Princeton, shielding her, is a ring of silence—certified milk dairies, great estates with peacocks and deer parks, pleasant farms and woodlands which we paced off and mapped down in the spring of 1917 in preparation for the war. The busy East has already dropped away when the branch train rattles familiarly from the junction. Two tall spires and then suddenly all around you spreads out the loveliest riot of Gothic architecture in America, battlement linked on to battlement, hall to hall, arch-broken, vine-covered—luxuriant and lovely over two square miles of green grass. Here is no monotony, no feeling that it was all built yesterday at the whim of last week's millionaire; Nassau Hall was already twenty years old when Hessian bullets pierced its sides.

Alfred Noyes has compared Princeton to Oxford. To me the two are sharply different. Princeton is thinner and fresher, at once less profound and more elusive. For all its past, Nassau Hall stands there hollow and barren, not like a mother who has borne sons and wears the scars of her travail but like a patient old nurse, skeptical and affectionate with these foster children who, as Americans, can belong to no place under the sun.

In my romantic days I tried to conjure up the Princeton of Aaron Burr, Philip Freneau, James Madison and Light-Horse Harry Lee, to tie on, so to speak, to the eighteenth century, to the history of man. But the chain parted at the Civil War, always the broken link in the continuity of American life. Colonial Princeton was, after all, a small denominational college. The Princeton I knew and belonged to grew from President McCosh's great shadow in the seventies, grew with the great *post bellum* fortunes of New York and Philadelphia to include coaching parties and keg parties and the later American conscience and Booth Tarkington's Triangle Club and Wilson's cloistered plans for an educational utopia. Bound up with it somewhere was the rise of American football.

For at Princeton, as at Yale, football became, back in the nineties, a sort of symbol. Symbol of what? Of the eternal violence of American life? Of the eternal immaturity of the race? The failure of a culture within the walls? Who knows? It became something at first satisfactory, then essential and beautiful. It became, long before the insatiable millions took it, with Gertrude Ederle and Mrs. Snyder, to its heart, the most intense and dramatic spectacle since the Olympic games. The death of Johnny Poe with the Black Watch in Flanders starts the cymbals crashing for me, plucks the strings of nervous violins as no adventure of the mind that Princeton ever offered. A year ago in the Champs-Élysées I passed a slender, dark-haired young man with an indolent characteristic walk. Something stopped inside me; I turned and looked after him. It was the romantic Buzz Law whom I had last seen one cold fall twilight in 1913, kicking from behind his goal line with a bloody bandage round his head.

After the beauty of its towers and the drama of its arenas, the widely known feature of Princeton is its "clientele."

A large proportion of such gilded youth as will absorb an education drifts to Princeton. Goulds, Rockefellers, Harrimans, Morgans, Fricks, Firestones, Perkinses, Pynes, McCormicks, Wanamakers, Cudahys and DuPonts light there for a season, well or less well regarded. The names of Pell, Biddle, Van Rensselaer, Stuyvesant, Schuyler and Cooke titillate second generation mammas and papas with a social row to hoe in Philadelphia or New York. An average class is composed of three dozen boys from such Midas academies as St. Paul's, St. Mark's, St. George's, Pomfret and Groton, a hundred and fifty more from Lawrenceville, Hotchkiss, Exeter, Andover and Hill, and perhaps another two hundred from less widely known preparatory schools. The remaining twenty per cent enter from the high schools and these last furnish a large proportion of the eventual leaders. For them the business of getting to Princeton has been more arduous, financially as well as scholastically. They are trained and eager for the fray.

In my time, a decade ago, the mid-winter examinations in freshman year meant a great winnowing. The duller athletes, the rich boys of thicker skulls than their forebears, fell in droves by the wayside. Often they had attained the gates at twenty or twenty-one and with the aid of a tutoring school only to find the first test too hard. They were usually a pleasant fifty or sixty, those first flunk-outs. They left many regrets behind.

Nowadays only a few boys of that caliber ever enter. Under the new system of admissions they are spotted by their early scholastic writhings and balkings and informed that Princeton has space only for those whose brains are of normal weight. This is because a few years ago the necessity arose of limiting the enrollment. The war prosperity made college possible for many boys and by 1921 the number of candidates, who each year satisfied the minimum scholastic requirements for Princeton, was far beyond the university's capacity.

So, in addition to the college board examinations, the candidate must present his scholastic record, the good word of his schools, of two Princeton alumni, and must take a psychological test for general intelligence. The six hundred or so who with these credentials make the most favorable impression on the admissions committee are admitted. A man who is deficient in one scholastic subject may succeed in some cases over a man who has passed them all. A boy with a really excellent record, in, say, science and mathematics, and a poor one in English, is admitted in preference to a boy with a fair general average and no special aptitude. The plan has raised the standard of scholarship and kept out such men as A, who in my time turned up in four different classes as a sort of perennial insult to the intelligence.

Whether the proverbially narrow judgments of head masters upon adolescents will serve to keep out the

Goldsmiths, the Byrons, the Whitmans and the O'Neills is too early to tell.

I can't help hoping that a few disreputable characters will slip in to salt the salt of the earth. Priggishness sits ill on Princeton. It was typified in my day by the Polity Club. This was a group that once a fortnight sat gravely at the feet of Mr. Schwab or Judge Gary or some other parietal-like spirit imported for the occasion. Had these inspired plutocrats disclosed trade secrets or even remained on the key of brisk business cynicism the occasion might have retained dignity, but the Polity Club were treated to the warmed over straw soup of the house organ and the production picnic, with a few hot sops thrown in about "future leaders of men." Looking through a copy of the latest year book I do not find the Polity Club at all. Perhaps it now serves worthier purposes.

President Hibben is a mixture of "normalcy" and discernment, of staunch allegiance to the *status quo* and of a fine tolerance amounting almost to intellectual curiosity. I have heard him in a speech mask with rhetoric statements of incredible shallowness; yet I have never known him to take a mean, narrow or short-sighted stand within Princeton's walls. He fell heir to the throne in 1912 during the reaction to the Wilson idealism, and I believe that, learning vicariously, he has pushed out his horizon amazingly since then. His situation was not unlike Harding's ten years later, but, surrounding himself with such men as Gauss, Heermance and Alexander Smith, he has abjured the merely passive and conducted a progressive and often brilliant administration.

Under him functions a fine philosophy department; an excellent department of classics, fathered by the venerable Dean West; a scientific faculty starred by such names as Oswald Veblen and Conklin; and a surprisingly pallid English department, top-heavy, undistinguished and with an uncanny knack of making literature distasteful to young men. Dr. Spaeth, one of several exceptions, coached the crew in the afternoon and in the mornings aroused interest and even enthusiasm for the romantic poets, an interest later killed in the preceptorial rooms where mildly poetic gentlemen resented any warmth of discussion and called the prominent men of the class by their first names.

The "Nassau Literary Magazine" is the oldest college publication in America. In its files you can find the original Craig Kennedy story, as well as prose or poetry by Woodrow Wilson, John Grier Hibben, Henry van Dyke, David Graham Phillips, Stephen French Whitman, Booth Tarkington, Struthers Burt, Jesse Lynch Williams— almost every Princeton writer save Eugene O'Neill. To Princeton's misfortune, O'Neill's career terminated by request three years too soon. The "Princetonian," the daily, is a conventional enough affair, though its editorial policy occasionally embodies coherent ideas, notably under James Bruce, Forrestal and John Martin, now of "Time." The "Tiger," the comic, is, generally speaking, inferior to the "Lampoon," the "Record" and the "Widow." When it was late to press, John Biggs and I used to write whole issues in the interval between darkness and dawn.

The Triangle Club (acting, singing and dancing) is Princeton's most characteristic organization. Founded by Booth Tarkington with the production of his libretto, "The Honorable Julius Caesar," it blooms in a dozen cities every Christmastide. On the whole it represents a remarkable effort and under the wing of Donald Clive Stuart, it has become, unlike the Mask and Wig Club of Pennsylvania, entirely an intramural affair. Its best years have been due to the residence of such talented improvisers as Tarkington, Roy Durstine, Walker Ellis, Ken Clark, or Erdman Harris. In my day it had a rowdy side but now the inebriated comedians and the all-night rehearsals are no more. It furnishes a stamping ground for the multiplying virtuosos of jazz, and the competition for places in the cast and chorus testifies to its popularity and power.

Princeton's sacred tradition is the honor system, a method of pledging that to the amazement of outsiders actually works, with consequent elimination of suspicion and supervision. It is handed over as something humanly precious to the freshmen within a week of their entrance. Personally I have never seen or heard of a Princeton man cheating in an examination, though I am told a few such cases have been mercilessly and summarily dealt with. I can think of a dozen times when a page of notes glanced at in a wash room would have made the difference between failure and success for me, but I can't recall any moral struggles in the matter. It simply doesn't occur to you, any more than it would occur to you to rifle your roommate's pocketbook. Perhaps the thing that struck deepest in the last autumn's unfortunate "Lampoon" was the mention of the honor system with an insinuation and a sneer.

No freshmen allowed on Prospect Street; these are the eighteen upper class clubs. I first heard of them in an article by, I think, Owen Johnson, in "Collier's" nearly twenty years ago. Pictures of Ivy, Cottage, Tiger Inn, and Cap and Gown smiled from the page not like the tombs of robber barons on the Rhine but like friendly and distinguished havens where juniors and seniors might eat three semiprivate meals a day. Later I remember Prospect Street as the red torchlight of the freshman parade flickered over the imposing façades of the houses and the white shirt fronts of the upper classmen, and gleamed in the champagne goblets raised to toast the already prominent members of my class.

There are no fraternities at Princeton; toward the end of each year the eighteen clubs take in an average of about twenty-five sophomores each, seventy-five per cent of the class. The remaining twenty-five per cent continue to eat in the university dining halls and this situation has been the cause of revolutions, protests, petitions, and innumerable editorials in the "Alumni Weekly." But the clubs represent an alumni investment of two million dollars—the clubs remain.

The Ivy Club was founded in 1879 and four years out of every five it is the most coveted club in Princeton. Its prestige is such that, broadly speaking, it can invite twenty boys out of every class and get fifteen of them. Not infrequently it has its debacles. Cottage, Tiger Inn or Cap and Gown—these three with Ivy have long been known as the "big" clubs—will take ten or fifteen of the boys that Ivy wants and Ivy will be left with a skeleton section of a dozen and considerable bitterness toward its successful rivals. The University Cottage Club, feared and hated politically, has made several such raids. Architecturally the most sumptuous of the clubs, Cottage was founded in 1886. It has a large Southern following, particularly in St. Louis and Baltimore. Unlike these two, Tiger Inn cultivates a bluff simplicity. Its membership is largely athletic and while it pretends to disdain social qualifications it has a sharp exclusiveness of its own. The fourth big club, Cap and Gown, began as an organization of earnest and somewhat religious young men, but during the last ten years social and political successes have overshadowed its original purpose. As late as 1916 its president could still sway a wavering crowd of sophomores with the happy slogan of "Join Cap and Gown and Meet God."

Of the others Colonial, an old club with a history of ups and downs, Charter, a comparative newcomer, and Quadrangle, the only club with a distinctly intellectual flavor, are the most influential. One club vanished in the confusion of the war. Two have been founded since, both of them in a little old building which has seen the birth of many. The special characteristics of the clubs vary so that it is hazardous to describe them. One, whose members in my day were indefatigable patrons of the Nassau Inn Bar, is now, I am told, a sort of restaurant for the Philadelphian Society.

The Philadelphian Society is Princeton's Y.M.C.A., and in more sagacious moments it is content to function as such. Occasionally, though, it becomes inspired with a Messianic urge to evangelize the university. In my day, for example, it imported for the purpose a noted rabble rouser, one Dr. X, who brought along in all seriousness a reformed Bad Example. Such students as out of piety or curiosity could be assembled were herded into Alexander Hall and there ensued one of the most grotesque orgies ever held in the shadow of a great educational institution. When Dr. X's sermon had risen to an inspirational chant, several dozen boys rose, staunch as colored gentlemen, and went forward to be saved. Among them was a popular free thinker and wine bibber whose sincerity we later probed but never determined. The climax of the occasion was the Bad Example's account of his past excesses, culminating in his descent into an actual stone gutter, his conversion and his rise to the position of Bad Example for Dr. X's traveling circus.

By this time the tenderer spirits in the audience had become uncomfortable, the tougher ones riotous; a few left the hall. The unctuousness of the proceedings was too much even for those more timorous days, and later there were protests on the grounds of sheer good taste. Last year "Buchmanism," a milder form of the same melodrama, came in for some outspoken and impatient criticism in the university press.

There is so much of Princeton that I have omitted

to touch. Perhaps to be specific for a moment will be a method of being most general. Vivid lights played on the whole colorful picture during the winter and early spring of 1917, just before the war.

Never had the forces which compose the university been so strong and so in evidence. Four score sophomores had democratically refused to join clubs, under the leadership of David Bruce (a son of Senator Bruce), Richard Cleveland (a son of President Cleveland), and Henry Hyacinth Strater of Louisville, Kentucky. Not content with this, the latter, the first man in his class to make the "Princetonian" and an ardent devotee of Tolstoy and Edward Carpenter, came out as a pacifist. He was brilliant and deeply popular; he was much patronized, somewhat disapproved of but never in the slightest degree persecuted. He made a few converts who joined the Quakers and remained pacifists to the end.

The "Nassau Literary Magazine" under John Peale Bishop made a sudden successful bid for popular attention. Jack Newlin, later killed in France, drew Beardsley-like pictures for frontispieces; I wrote stories about current prom girls, stories that were later incorporated into a novel; John Biggs imagined the war with sufficient virtuosity to deceive veterans; and John Bishop made a last metrical effort to link up the current crusade with the revolution—while we all, waiting to go to training camps, found time heartily to despise the bombast and rhetoric of the day. We published a satirical number, a parody on the "Cosmopolitan Magazine," which infuriated the less nimble-witted members of the English department. We—this time the board of the "Tiger"—issued an irreverent number which burlesqued the faculty, the anticlub movement and then the clubs themselves, by their real names. Everything around us seemed to be breaking up. These were the great days; battle was on the horizon; nothing was ever going to be the same again and nothing mattered. And for the next two years nothing did matter. Five per cent of my class, twenty-one boys, were killed in the war.

That spring I remember late nights at the Nassau Inn with Bill Coan, the proctor, waiting outside to hail selected specimens before the dean next morning. I remember the long afternoons of military drill on the soccer fields, side by side perhaps with an instructor of the morning. We used to snicker at Professor Wardlaw Miles' attempts to reconcile the snap of the drill manual with his own precise and pedantic English. There were no snickers two years later when he returned from France with a leg missing and his breast bright with decorations. A thousand boys cheered him to his home. I remember the last June night when, with two-thirds of us in uniform, our class sang its final song on the steps of Nassau Hall and some of us wept because we knew we'd never be quite so young any more as we had been here. And I seem to remember a host of more intimate things that are now as blurred and dim as our cigarette smoke or the ivy on Nassau Hall that last night.

Princeton is itself. Williams College is not "what Princeton used to be." Williams is for guided boys whose female relatives want them protected from reality. Princeton is of the world; it is somehow on the "grand scale"; and for sixty years it has been approximately the same. There is less singing and more dancing. The keg parties are over but the stags line up for a hundred yards to cut in on young Lois Moran. There is no Elizabethan Club as at Yale to make a taste for poetry respectable, sometimes too respectable; exceptional talent must create its own public at Princeton, as it must in life. In spite of all persuasions the varsity man conservatively wears his P on the inside of his sweater, but so far no Attorney General Palmers or Judge Thayers have bobbed up among the alumni. President Hibben sometimes disagrees aloud with Secretary Mellon and only ninety-two members of the senior class proclaimed themselves dry last year.

Looking back over a decade one sees the ideal of a university become a myth, a vision, a meadow lark among the smoke stacks. Yet perhaps it is there at Princeton, only more elusive than under the skies of the Prussian Rhineland or Oxfordshire; or perhaps some men come upon it suddenly and possess it, while others wander forever outside. Even these seek in vain through middle age for any corner of the republic that preserves so much of what is fair, gracious, charming and honorable in American life.

—*College Humor*, **December 1927**

A Short Autobiography
(with acknowledgements to Nathan)

1913

The four defiant Canadian Club whiskeys at the Susque-
hanna in Hackensack.

1914

The Great Western Champagne at the Trent House in
Trenton and the groggy ride back to Princeton.

1915

The Sparkling Burgundy at Bustanoby's. The raw whiskey in White Sulphur Springs, Montana, when I got up
on a table and sang "Won't you come up," to the cowmen.
The Stingers at Tate's in Seattle listening to Ed Muldoon,
"that clever chap."

1916

The apple brandy nipped at in the locker room at the
White Bear Yacht Club.

1917

A first Burgundy with Monsignor X at the Lafayette. Blackberry Brandy and Whiskey with Tom at the old Nassau Inn.

1918

The Bourbon smuggled to officers' rooms by bellboys at the Seelbach Hotel in Louisville.

1919

The Sazerac Cocktails brought up from New Orleans to Montgomery to celebrate an important occasion.

1920

Red wine at Mollat's. Absinthe cocktails in a hermetically sealed apartment in the Royalton. Corn liquor by moonlight in a deserted aviation field in Alabama.

1921

Leaving our Champagne in the Savoy Grill on the Fourth of July when a drunk brought up two obviously Piccadilly ladies. Yellow Chartreuse in the Via Balbini in Rome.

1922

Kaly's crème de cacao cocktails in St. Paul. My own first and last manufacture of gin.

1923

Oceans of Canadian Ale with R. Lardner in Great Neck, Long Island.

1924

Champagne cocktails on the *Minnewaska* and apologizing to the old lady we kept awake. Graves Kressman at Villa Marie in Valescure and consequent arguments about British politics with the nursery governess. Porto Blancs at a time of sadness. Mousseux bought by a Frenchman in a garden at twilight. Chambéry Fraise with the Seldes on their honeymoon. The local product ordered on the wise advice of a friendly priest at Orvieto, when we were asking for French wines.

1925

A dry white wine that "won't travel," made a little South of Sorrento, that I've never been able to trace. Plot coagulating—a sound of hoofs and bugles. The gorgeous Vin d'Arbois at La Reine Pédauque. Champagne cocktails in the Ritz sweatshop in Paris. Poor wines from Nicolas. Kirsch in a Burgundy inn against the rain with E. Hemingway.

1926

Uninteresting St. Estèphe in a desolate hole called Salies-de-Béarn. Sherry on the beach at La Garoupe. Gerald M.'s grenadine cocktail, the one flaw to make everything perfect in the world's most perfect house. Beer and weenies with Grace, Charlie, Ruth and Ben at Antibes before the deluge.

1927

Delicious California "Burgundy-type" wine in one of the Ambassador bungalows in Los Angeles. The beer I made in Delaware that had a dark inescapable sediment. Cases of dim, cut, unsatisfactory whiskey in Delaware.

1928

The Pouilly with Bouillabaisse at Prunier's in a time of discouragement.

1929

A feeling that all liquor has been drunk and all it can do for one has been experienced, and yet—"*Garçon, un Chablis-Mouton 1902, et pour commencer, une petite carafe de vin rosé. C'est ça—merci.*"

—*New Yorker,* May 25, 1929

Girls Believe in Girls

I

Back in 1912 the Castles, by making modern dancing respectable, brought the nice girl into the cabaret and sat her down next to the distinctly not-nice girl—at that moment the Era of the Flapper was born. Some ten commandments crashed in the confusion of the war, and afterwards there was a demand not to be let down from its excitement. There were books that extended the possibilities of freedom and there was a generation educated entirely by women, and hence malleable, who simply flowed out to the new horizons of the pre-war liberals. By about 1922 youth had been thoroughly converted, or as some reactionaries said perverted, and the fun went out of it—the "flapper movement" proper was over.

But had the movement ever been really unsentimental, a real facing of anything, except a little questionable biological data? (It is, for instance, doubtful whether a protracted physical courtship is a normal or healthy introduction to marriage, particularly for men.) On the contrary, the young girl making a present of herself to a swain stuck pretty close to the fictional pattern. She was Thackeray's Beatrix Esmond who, in 1912, turned up again in Wells' "Tono-Bungay" under the name Beatrice Normandy and was passionately emulated by a very select and daring crop of London debutantes. The fascinating

109

Beatrice begot the ladies of Michael Arlen and of almost everyone else who dealt in heroic English girls—but I think the adolescent group in Chicago who about 1915 discovered the automobile were more nearly a spontaneous apparition. Anyhow by the end of the war, the whole thing was so drippy with sentimentality that the sob sisters got their teeth into it and the crowd took it up, and with the crowd there ran a woman of forty-four, a bit out of breath, in whom the flapper was somewhat surprised to recognize her own mother.

It was finished—yesterday's fashion, heavens, how horrible! Marching with the advance guard was one thing, trailing along with the herd was another, and straight-away individualism was born and with it the modern and somewhat disturbing cult of the heroine.

Before speaking of this it is well to remember that a true generation, one which forms a clearly marked type and is stamped with a certain unanimity of conduct and opinion, doesn't appear every three or four years. Roughly speaking the girls who were or would have been debutantes in 1917–1919 were the nucleus of the wild generation—their numbers were swollen by older and younger girls who were determined not to miss anything, for the wild ones seemed to be having a good time. It is dispersed now to the country club, the European casino, the stage and even the home, and is passing its thirtieth birthday. There may not be another such generation until there is a new war or new limits marked out for new youth to surge into and fill. For youth is not original—remove the automobile and the bottom drops out of the whole hilarious spectacle which has amused the nation for a decade. The monkey strapped to a bicycle is after all without significance. What is worth examining is a changing of the heart.

II

When I was very young, many older girls still kept theatrical scrap books and waited by the stage door after matinées to see Elsie Janis or Ethel Barrymore come out. Maybe the cult of the heroine is an accentuated and intensified development of that, but I do not think so. I think women have come to believe that they have nothing of value to learn from men. Generally speaking the man of intelligence either runs alone, or seeks amusement in stimulating circles—in any case he is rarely available; the business man brings to social intercourse little more than what he reads in the papers, together with a passionate desire to be entertained; so that in the thousand and one women's worlds that cover the land, the male voice is represented largely by the effeminate and the weak, the parasite and the failure. That the first of these groups has increased in size since the war is notorious. Certain words describing certain types are in everyone's vocabulary. Scarcely a popular woman in a large city but hasn't one or two in tow who can be counted on to take her part, appreciate her clothes, keep the ball of gossip rolling—and, especially, to be available.

If a somewhat bizarre locality can be put in evidence, one finds in Los Angeles a host of often charming and almost always pretty women partnered by countless actors, profile boys, costume designers, hangers-on and people's brothers—with the addition of a few exceptionally tough-skinned business men on Saturday and Sunday nights. At how many parties have I watched the attractive girls slip quietly away to talk and joke with each other in the wash room, bored and impatient with such a world of men. And in the country at large a parallel mood exists.

With the general confusion as to what men want—"Shall I be fast or shall I be straight? Shall I help him succeed or join him only after he has? Shall I settle down or shall I keep young? Shall I have one child or four?"—these problems, once confined to certain classes, being now every girl's problems—they have begun to turn for approval not to men but to each other. "Crushes" were once a boarding-school phenomenon—now any sort of courageous individualism makes a woman the center of a cult. Not only do Edna Millay, Helen Wills, Geraldine Farrar, and the Queen of Roumania have their disciples, but there are passionately admiring voices for Aimee Semple McPherson and even Ruth Snyder. What effect has this woman worship on the young girl herself?

She is quieter—lest other girls might think her rowdy, and with the same idea in mind she has grown increasingly polite. She wants to be considered simple and sincere because among girls emphasis is put on these qualities. She drinks less, save in the bored South and Middle West where it is still the fashion. She knows "something about music" but is less likely to be a virtuoso of the piano, because while one plays for men, one talks about it for women. She knows something about calories but nothing about cooking, and for the same reason. Yet she would gladly take up these things were she a little surer they led to distinction. Distinction is everything—not merely the distinction of Clara Bow but the distinction of Madame Curie. It is the old American idealism but functioning well outside the no longer all-absorbing home,—restlessly seeking women Messiahs but indifferent to the self-appointed stuffed chemises of public life and grown skeptical about the causes for which their elders have battled these twenty years—and so by a curious reaction become conservative, become "cagey," waiting to see.

On the Riviera last summer there were English girls who still believed in men—you could tell by the deliberate outdoor swagger of their walk, by what they laughed at so heartily, as if they were still apologizing for having been born girls, and were being "good chaps" for critical elder brothers. But as for the others—you could only tell the Americans from the French because they were pretty—the negligence with which they obviously took their men was almost shocking. Outside of material matters man's highest and most approved incarnation was as "a good old horse," be he fiancé, husband or lover. The merely masculine was considered by turns stuffy, dull, tyrannical or merely ludicrous. I remember a girl responding to a desirable middle-aged party's inquiry as to whether he could smoke a cigar with: "Please do. There's nothing I like so much as a good cigar."—and I remember the suppressed roar of hilarity that circled the table. It was the voice of another age—it was burlesque. Naturally one wanted and needed men, but wanting to please them, positively *coddling* them in that fashion—that was another matter.

The Prince, the Hero, no longer exists, or rather fails to put in an appearance, for society with its confusion and its wide-open doors no longer offers the stability of thirty years ago. In New York it has been difficult for years to arrange a numerical superiority of men over women at debutante balls. All the young girl can be sure of when she comes out into "the world" is that she will meet plenty of males competent to stimulate her biological urges—for the heterogeneous stag-line can do that if nothing more.

Her current attitude toward moral questions is that of the country at large—in other words the identification of virtue with chastity no longer exists among girls over twenty, and to pretend it does is just one of those things you are welcome to do if it gives you comfort. There are those of an older and purer generation who would have liked the present observer to have devoted his entire article to this phenomenon—and at the end virtuously thrown the magazine out the window. For America is composed not of two sorts of people, but of two frames of mind—the first engaged in doing what it would like to do, the second pretending that such things do not exist. It is obvious to the most casually honest glance that we have taken over in its entirety the French lightness about sexual matters, in speech and in deed, with the difference that in America this lightness extends to the young girl.

She is quieter about her rules of conduct, much less blatant and boastful than was her flapper sister—and I am reminded that back in the days of unbelievable inhibitions the girls who really "necked" didn't talk about it. Difficult as it is to make generalities, it is apparent through the thinning smoke that most of the barriers are pretty definitely down. Men, being reduced in the great national matriarchy to love-making animals, need no longer be considered in their masterful, priestly and retributive aspect, demanding accounts, and passing judgments, for then they are merely "being stupid"—and who cares anyhow? There are increasing thousands of girls who choose to go their way alone.

Besides, the contemporary girl has thrown a mantle of good taste over much that was previously offensive. Absorbing manners from both her pre-war mother and her post-war sister she has chosen something from each, and wandering over Europe, she displays a poise and self-confidence that makes the English girl seem immature, and the French girl rigid and harsh. At this moment she is our finest and most representative product from the point of view of beauty, charm and courage, and it seems positively disloyal to wonder if progress does finally culminate in her insouciant promenade along the narrow steel girder of our prosperity. Yet the question remains whether any type so exquisitely achieved, so perennially unworried, will accomplish anything at all.

III

It is not my question—I expect wonders of them, literally. It is the poor young man I worry about—in such time as all but professional worriers spare for such matters. From the international circus on the Riviera, one picks out the perfect flower of every race—the dark little Greek with a head by Praxiteles, the sun-colored Neapolitan virgin, the rose-pink Briton, the svelte Parisienne—and she turns out generally to be Miss Mary Meriwether of Paris, Michigan, or Athens, Georgia—triumphantly and gratifyingly ours. To them the world is not the romantic mystery it was to us—even the past throws no shadow, since they believe in nobody but themselves. Such loveliness cannot lack a voice to express it, nor such courage a way to spend itself—and, turning the medal, one guesses that such intolerable success will drive the defeated and repressed ones to justify themselves passionately by achievement. Something dynamic and incalculable that has always been inherent in American life, even when it was reduced to the fretful whine of the frontier woman, something that failed to fulfill itself in either the sentimental Gibson Girl, or the rowdy flapper, seems to have broken through the egg at last—and come into its own.

—*Liberty*, February 8, 1930

Salesmanship in
the Champs-Élysées

To work for the Company Automobile is a *métier* exact-
ing. There of them are many of the world who, wanting to purchase an automobile, enter and say "I want to
purchase an automobile," whereupon this affair begins.
Now one has at the outset the information that this man
wishes well to purchase a car and has already decided on
this mark—otherwise he would not have entered here.
One can then, naturally, amuse oneself by for a moment
mocking of him, giving him to wonder if of them there
are after all. During this quarter of an hour one can dis-
cover much of the type with which one is dealing at the
moment and thus in any further dealing one has provided
himself with resources or even established a certain dominance of character, one on top of the other.

It there has been several days when an American
entered and demanded me to make him see a car. I was
engaged standing in a spot thinking of affairs of one's
own; presently I demanded:

"What is it that it is?"

"A car."

"A six-cylinder touring car."

"We have not one here."

I had the man there, and for a moment he looked stu-
pefied—but then he made:

"Can you have one here for me to see this afternoon?"

This fantastic request I only answered with a bitter and short laugh.

"And how much is it?" he continued. "As a matter of fact I'm pretty sure I want one, so I can write you a cheque."

This was becoming wearying. I drew in my breath and made: "Listen, monsieur, it is not the trouble to talk when I have told you I have now no car of that kind in the house. Nothing! Nothing! Nothing! It does not exist here. Look for yourself."

"When will you have?"

"How should I know? Perhaps in eight days. Perhaps in a month."

"I don't think you want to sell me a car," he said. "As a matter of fact they carry a make next door that I begin to think will do just as well."

He turned and went out suddenly and I stood looking after the impolite. But thinking to profit himself he is in the end deceived, because Mr. Legoupy, the seller next door, will no more sell him without making a proper study of his sincerity and his character and the extent of his desire for the car than I myself. The impolite will end himself by being able to get no car at all.

—*New Yorker,* 15 February 1930

The Death of My Father

(unfinished)

Convention would make me preface this with an apology for the lack of taste of discussing an emotion so close to me. But all my criteria of taste disappeared when I read Mrs. Emily Price Post's Book of Etiquette some months ago. Up to that time I had always thought of myself as an American gentleman, somewhat crazy and often desperate and bad but partaking of the sensitivity of my race and class and with a record of many times having injured the strong but never the weak. But now I don't know—the mixture of the obvious and the snobbish in that book—and it's an honest book, a frank piece of worldly wisdom written for the new women of the bull market—has sent me back again to all the things I felt at twenty. I kept wondering all through it how Mrs. Post would have thought of my father.

I loved my father—always deep in my subconscious I have referred judgments back to him, to what he would have thought or done. He loved me—and felt a deep responsibility for me—I was born several months after the sudden death of my two elder sisters and he felt what the effect of this would be on my mother, that he would be my only moral guide. He became that to the best of his ability. He came from tired old stock with very little left of vitality and mental energy but he managed to raise a little for me.

We walked downtown in the summer to have our shoes shined, me in my sailor suit and Father in his always beautifully cut clothes, and he told me the few things I ever learned about life until a few years later from a Catholic priest, Monsignor Fay. What he knew he had learned from his mother and grandmother, the latter a bore to me—"If your Grandmother Scott heard that she would turn over in her grave." What he told me were simple things.

"Once when I went in a room as a young man I was confused, so I went up to the oldest woman there and introduced myself and afterwards the people of that town always thought I had good manners." He did that from a good heart that came from another America—he was much too sure of what he was, much too sure of the deep pride of the two proud women who brought him up, to doubt for a moment that his own instincts were good. It was a horror to find the natural gesture expressed with cynical distortion in Mrs. Price Post's book.

We walked downtown in Buffalo on Sunday mornings and my white ducks were stiff with starch and he was very proud walking with his handsome little boy. We had our shoes shined and he lit his cigar and we bought the Sunday papers. When I was a little older I did not understand at all why men that I knew were vulgar and not gentlemen made him stand up or give the better chair on our verandah. But I know now. There was new young peasant stock coming up every ten years and he was of the generation of the colonies and the revolution.

Once he hit me. I called him a liar—I was about thirteen, I think, and I said if he called me a liar he was a liar. He hit me—he had spanked me before and always with good reason, but this time there was ill feeling and we were both sorry for years, I think, though we didn't say anything to each other. Later we used to have awful rows on political subjects on which we violently disagreed but we never came to the point of personal animosity about them but if things came to fever heat the one most affected quitted the arena, left the room.

I don't see how all this could possibly interest anyone but me.

I ran away when I was seven on the Fourth of July— I spent the day with a friend in a pear orchard and the police were informed that I was missing and on my return my father thrashed me according to the custom of the nineties—on the bottom—and then let me come out and watch the night fireworks from the balcony with my pants still down and my behind smarting and knowing in my heart that he was absolutely right. Afterwards, seeing in his face his regret that it had to happen, I asked him to tell me a story. I knew what it would be—he had only a few, the story of the spy, the one about the man hung up by his thumbs, the one about Early's march.

Do you want to hear them? I'm so tired of them all that I can't make them interesting. But maybe they are because I used to ask Father to repeat and repeat and repeat.

—*The Princeton University Library Chronicle,*
Summer 1951

This unfinished essay was composed by Fitzgerald shortly after his father's death on January 26, 1931. It was found among his papers after his own death in 1940 and was first published in the *Princeton University Library Chronicle*, Summer 1951. That text is published here.

One Hundred False Starts

Crack! goes the pistol and off starts this entry. Sometimes he has caught it just right, more often he has jumped the gun. On these occasions if he is lucky he runs only a dozen yards, looks around and jogs sheepishly back to the starting place. But too frequently he makes the entire circuit of the track under the impression that he is leading the field and reaches the finish to find he has no following. The race must be run all over again.

A little more training, take a long walk, cut out that night-cap, no meat at dinner, and stop worrying about politics—

So runs an interview with one of the champion false-starters of the writing profession—myself. Opening a leather-bound scrap-basket which I fatuously refer to as my "note-book," I pick out at random a small triangular piece of wrapping paper with a cancelled stamp on one side. On the other side is written:

Boopsie Dee was cute.

Nothing more. No cue as to what was intended to follow that preposterous statement. Boopsie Dee, indeed! confronting me with this single dogmatic fact about herself. Never will I know what happened to her, where and when she picked up her revolting name, and whether her cuteness got her into much trouble.

121

I pick out another scrap:

*Article—"Unattractive Things Girls Do," to pair with
counter article by woman: "Unattractive Things Men
Do."*
No. 1 Remove glass eye at dinner table.

That's all there is on that scrap. Evidently an idea that
had dissolved into hilarity before it had fairly got under
way. I try to revive it seriously. What unattractive things
do girls do? I mean universally nowadays. Or what unattractive things do a great majority of them do, or a strong
minority? I have a few feeble ideas but no, the notion
is dead. I can only think of an article I read somewhere
about a woman who divorced her husband because of the
way he stalked a chop, and wondering at the time why
she didn't try him out on a chop before she married him.
No, that all belongs to a gilded age when people could
afford to have nervous breakdowns because of the squeak
in Daddy's shoes.

There are hundreds of these hunches—not all of
them have to do with literature. Some are hunches about
importing a troupe of Ouled Nail dancers from Africa,
about bringing the Grand Guignol from Paris to New
York, about resuscitating football at Princeton (I have two
scoring plays that will make a coach's reputation in one
season), and there is a faded note to "explain to D. W.
Griffith why costume plays are sure to come back." Also
my plan for a film version of H. G. Wells's "History of the
World."

These little flurries caused me no travail—they were
opium eaters' illusions, vanishing with the smoke of the
pipe, or you know what I mean. The pleasure of thinking
about them was the exact equivalent of having accom-
plished them. It is the six-page, ten-page, thirty-page

globs of paper that grieve me professionally, like unsuccessful oil shafts—they represent my false starts.

There is, for example, one false start which I have made at least a dozen times. It is, or rather has tried to take shape as, a short story. At one time or another I have written as many words on it as would make a presentable novel, yet the present version is only about twenty-five hundred words long and hasn't been touched for two years. Its present name—it has gone under various aliases—is "The Barnaby Family."

From childhood I have had a day-dream—what a word for one whose entire life is spent noting them down—about starting at scratch on a desert island and building a comparatively high state of civilization out of the materials at hand. I always felt that Robinson Crusoe cheated when he rescued the tools from the wreck, and this applies equally to the "Swiss Family Robinson," the "Two Little Savages" and the balloon castaways of "The Mysterious Island." In my story not only would no convenient grain of wheat, Winchester repeater, 4,000 H. P. Diesel Engine or technocratic butler be washed ashore, but even my characters would be helpless city-dwellers with no more wood-lore than a cuckoo out of a clock.

The creation of such characters was easy, and it was easy washing them ashore:

> For three long hours they were prostrated on the beach. Then Donald sat up:
>
> "Well, here we are," he said with sleepy vagueness.
>
> "Where?" his wife demanded eagerly.
>
> "It couldn't be America and it couldn't be the Philippines," he said, "because we started from one and haven't got to the other."
>
> "I'm thirsty," said the child.

Donald's eyes went quickly to the shore.

"Where's the raft?" He looked rather accusingly at Vivian. "Where's the raft?"

"It was gone when I woke up."

"It would be," he exclaimed bitterly. "Somebody might have thought of bringing the jug of water ashore. If I don't do it nothing is done in this house—I mean this family."

All right, go on from there. Anybody—you back there in the tenth row, step up! Don't be afraid—just go on with the story. If you get stuck you can look up tropical fauna and flora in the encyclopedia—or call up a neighbor who has been shipwrecked.

Anyhow that's the exact point where my story (and I still think it's a great plot) begins to creak and groan with unreality. I turn around after a while with a sense of uneasiness—how could anybody believe that rubbish about monkeys throwing cocoanuts—trot back to the starting place and I resume my crouch, for days and days.

During such days I sometimes examine a clot of pages which is headed "Ideas for possible stories." Among others I find the following:

Bathwater in Princeton or Florida.
Plot—suicide, indulgence, hate, liver and circumstance.
Snubbing or having somebody.
Dancer who found she could fly.

Oddly enough all these are intelligible if not enlightening suggestions to me. But they are all old, old—I am as apt to be stimulated by them as by my signature or the beat of my feet pacing the floor. There is one that for years has puzzled me, that is as great a mystery as Boopsie Dee.

STORY: THE WINTER WAS COLD

Characters
Victoria Cuomo
Mark de Vinci
Alice Hall
Jason Tenweather
Ambulance-surgeon
Stark, a watchman

What was this about? Who were these people with sinister names? I have no doubt that one of them was to be murdered or else be a murderee, and I can put my finger on the one—it was Victoria Cuomo. I know this because of my feeling for a certain Dr. Cuomo with whom I had some desperate dealings in Italy years ago. Undoubtedly I did not use that name without reason. But all else about the plot I have forgotten long ago.

I turn over a little. Here is something over which I linger longer—a false start that wasn't bad, that might have been run out.

WORDS

When you consider the more expensive article and finally decide on the cheaper one the salesman is usually thoughtful enough to make it all right for you. "You'll probably get the most wear out of this," he says consolingly. Or even, "That's the one I'd choose myself."

The Trimbles were like that. They were specialists in the neat promotion of the next best into the best.

"It'll do to wear around the house," they used to say, or "We want to wait until we can get a really nice one."

It was at this point that I decided I couldn't write about the Trimbles. They were very nice and I would have enjoyed somebody else's story of how they made out, but I couldn't get under the surface of their lives, what kept them content to make the best of things instead of changing things. So I gave them up.

There is the question of dog stories. I like dogs and would like to write at least one dog story in the style of Mr. Terhune, but see what happens when I take pen in hand:

"DOG"

The Story of a Little Dog

Only a newsboy with a wizened face selling his papers on the corner. A big dog-fancier standing on the curb laughed contemptuously and twitched up the collar of his airedale coat. Another rich dog-man gave a little bark of scorn from a passing taxi cab.

But the newsboy was interested in the animal that had crept close to his feet. He was only a cur—his fuzzy coat was inherited from his mother who had been a fashionable poodle while in stature he resembled his father, a great dane. And somewhere there was a canary concerned for a spray of yellow feathers projected from his backbone—

You see I couldn't go on like that. Think of dog owners writing in to the editors from all over the country protesting that I was no man for that job.

I am thirty-six years old. For eighteen years save for a short space during the war writing has been my chief interest in life, and I am in every sense a professional. Yet even now when, at the recurrent cry of "Baby Needs Shoes," I sit down facing my sharpened pencils and a block of legal-sized paper, I have a feeling of utter helplessness. I may write my story in three days or, as is more frequently the case, it may be six weeks before I have assembled anything worthy to be sent out. I can open a volume from a criminal law library and find a thousand plots. I can go into highway and byway, parlor and kitchen, and listen to personal revelations that at the hands of other writers might endure forever. But all that is nothing—not even enough for a false start.

Mostly we authors must repeat ourselves—that's the truth. We have two or three great and moving experiences in our lives, experiences so great and moving that it doesn't seem at the time that anyone else has been so caught up and pounded and dazzled and astonished and beaten and broken and rescued and illuminated and rewarded and humbled in just that way ever before. Then we learn our trade, well or less well, and we tell our two or three stories—each time in a new disguise— maybe ten times, maybe a hundred, as long as people will listen.

If this were otherwise one would have to confess to having no individuality at all. And each time I honestly believe that because I have found a new background and a novel twist, I have really got away from the two or three fundamental tales I have to tell. But it is rather like Ed Wynn's famous anecdote about the painter of boats who was begged to paint some ancestors for a client. The bargain was arranged but with the painter's final warning that the ancestors would all turn out to look like boats.

When I face the fact that all my stories are going to have a certain family resemblance I am taking a step toward avoiding false starts. If a friend says he's got a story for me and launches into a tale of being robbed by Brazilian pirates in a swaying straw hut on the edge of a smoking volcano in the Andes with his fiancée bound and gagged on the roof, I can well believe there were various human emotions involved; but having successfully avoided pirates, volcanoes and fiancées who get themselves bound and gagged on roofs, I can't feel them. Whether it's something that happened twenty years ago or only yesterday I must start out with an emotion, one that's close to me and that I can understand.

Last summer I was hauled to the hospital with high fever and a tentative diagnosis of typhoid. My affairs were in no better shape than yours are, reader—there was a story I should have written to pay my current debts, and I was haunted by the fact that I hadn't made a will. If I had really had typhoid I wouldn't have worried about such things, nor made that scene at the hospital when the nurses tried to plump me into an ice-bath. I didn't have either the typhoid or the bath but I continued to rail against my luck that just at this crucial moment I should have to waste two weeks in bed, answering the baby talk of nurses and getting nothing done at all. But three days after I was discharged I had finished a story about a hospital.

The material was soaking in and I didn't know it—I was profoundly moved by fear, apprehension, worry, impatience—every sense was acute and that is the best way of accumulating material for a story. Unfortunately it does not always come that easily. I say to myself (looking at the awful blank block of paper), "Now here's this man Swankins that I've known and liked for ten years. I am privy to all his private affairs, and some of them are wows. I've threatened to write about him and he says to go ahead and do my worst."

But can I? I've been in as many jams as Swankins but I didn't look at them the same way, nor would it ever have occurred to me to extricate myself from the Chinese police or from the clutches of that female in the way Swankins chose. I could write some fine paragraphs about Swankins, but build a story around him that would have an ounce of feeling in it—impossible.

Or into my distraught imagination wanders a girl named Elsie about whom I was almost suicidal for a month back in 1916.

"How about me?" Elsie says. "Surely you swore to a lot of emotion back there in the past. Have you forgotten?"

"No, Elsie, I haven't forgotten."

"Well then write a story about me. You haven't seen me for twelve years so you don't know how fat I am now and how boring I often seem to my husband."

"No, Elsie, I—"

"Oh come on—surely I must be worth a story. Why you used to hang around saying good-bye with your face so miserable and comic that I thought I'd go crazy myself before I got rid of you. And now you're afraid to even start a story about me. Your feeling must have been pretty thin if you can't revive it for a few hours."

"No, Elsie, you don't understand. I have written about you—a dozen times. That funny little rabbit curl to your lip I used in a story six years ago; that way your face all changed just when you were going to laugh—I gave that characteristic to one of the first girls I ever wrote about; the way I stayed around trying to say good-night, knowing that you'd rush to the phone as soon as the front door closed behind me—all that was in a book that I wrote once upon a time."

"I see. Just because I didn't respond to you, you broke me into bits and used me up piece-meal."

"I'm afraid so, Elsie. You see you never so much as kissed me, except that once with a kind of a shove at the same time, so there really isn't any story."

Plots without emotions—emotions without plots. So it goes sometimes. Let me suppose, however, that I have got under way—two days' work, two thousand words are finished and being typed for a first revision. And suddenly doubts overtake me.

What if I'm just horsing around? What's going on in this regatta anyhow? Who could care what happens to the girl, when the sawdust is obviously leaking out of her moment by moment? How did I get the plot all tangled up? I am alone in the privacy of my faded blue room with my sick cat, the bare February branches waving at the window, an ironic paper weight that says "Business Is Good," a New England Conscience (developed in Minnesota) and my greatest problem: "Shall I run it out? Or shall I turn back?" Shall I say:

"I know I had something to prove and it may develop farther along in the story," or else

"This is just bull-headedness—better throw it away and start over."

The latter is one of the most difficult decisions that an author must make—to make it philosophically before he has exhausted himself in a hundred-hour effort to resuscitate a corpse or disentangle innumerable wet snarls is a test of whether or not he is really a professional. There are often occasions when such a decision is doubly difficult—in the last stages of a novel for instance, when there is no question of junking the whole but where a whole favorite character has to be hauled out by the heels, screeching and dragging half a dozen good scenes with him.

It is here that these confessions tie up with a general problem as well as with those peculiar to a writer. The decision as to when to quit, as to when one is merely floundering around and causing other people trouble, has to be made frequently in a lifetime. In youth we are taught the rather simple rule never to quit, because we are presumably following programmes made by people wiser than ourselves. My own conclusion is that when one has embarked on a course that grows increasingly doubtful *and one feels the vital forces beginning to be used up*, it is best to ask advice if decent advice is within range. Columbus didn't and Lindbergh couldn't. So my statement at first seems heretical toward the idea that is pleasantest to live with—the idea of heroism. But I make a sharp division between one's professional life, when after the period of apprenticeship not more than ten per-cent of advice is worth a hoot, and one's private and worldly life, where often almost anyone's judgment is better than one's own.

Once, not so long ago when my work was hampered by so many false starts that I thought the game was up at last, and when my personal life was even more thoroughly obfuscated, I asked an old Alabama negro:

"Uncle Bob, when things get so bad that there isn't any way out, what do you do then?"

The heat from the kitchen stove stirred his white sideburns as he warmed himself. If I cynically expected a platitudinous answer, a reflection of something remembered from Uncle Remus, I was disappointed.

"Mr. Fitzgerald," he said, "when things get thataway I wuks."

It was good advice: work is almost everything. But it would be nice to be able to distinguish useful work from mere labor expended. Perhaps that is part of work itself—to find the difference. Perhaps my frequent solitary sprints around the track are profitable. Shall I tell you about another one? Very well. You see I had this hunch—but in counting the pages I find that my time is up and I must put my book of mistakes away. On the fire? No! I put it weakly back in the drawer. These old mistakes are now only toys, and expensive ones at that; give them a toy's cupboard and then hurry back into the serious business of my profession. Joseph Conrad defined it more clearly, more vividly than any man of our time:

"My task is by the power of the written word to make

you hear, to make you feel—it is, before all, to make you *see*."

It's not very difficult to run back and start over again—especially in private. What you aim at is to get in a good race or two when the crowd is in the stand.

—*Saturday Evening Post,* March 4, 1933

Author's House

I have seen numerous photographs and read many accounts of the houses of Joan Crawford, Virginia Bruce and Claudette Colbert, usually with the hostess done up from behind with a bib explaining how on God's earth to make a Hollywood soufflé or open a can of soup without removing the appendix in the same motion. But it has been a long time since I have seen a picture of an author's house and it occurs to me to supply the deficiency.

Of course I must begin with an apology for writing about authors at all. In the days of the old "Smart Set" Mencken and Nathan had a rejection slip which notified the aspirant that they would not consider stories about painters, musicians and authors—perhaps because these classes are supposed to express themselves fully in their own work and are not a subject for portraiture. And having made the timorous bow I proceed with the portrait.

Rather than leave a sombre effect at the end we begin at the bottom, in a dark damp unmodernized cellar. As your host's pale yellow flashlight moves slowly around through the spiderwebs, past old boxes and barrels and empty bottles and parts of old machines, you feel a little uneasy.

"Not a bad cellar—as cellars go," the author says. "You can't see it very well and I can't either—it's mostly forgotten."

"What do you mean?"

"It's everything I've forgotten—all the complicated dark mixture of my youth and infancy that made me a fiction writer instead of a fireman or a soldier. You see fiction is a trick of the mind and heart composed of as many separate emotions as a magician uses in executing a pass or a palm. When you've learned it you forget it and leave it down here."

"When did you learn it?"

"Oh every time I begin I have to learn it all over again in a way. But the intangibles are down here. Why I chose this God-awful *métier* of sedentary days and sleepless nights and endless dissatisfaction. Why I would choose it again. All that's down here and I'm just as glad I can't look at it too closely. See that dark corner?"

"Yes."

"Well, three months before I was born my mother lost her other two children and I think that came first of all though I don't know how it worked exactly. I think I started then to be a writer."

Your eyes fall on another corner and you give a start of alarm.

"What's that?" you demand.

"That?" The author tries to change the subject, moving around so as to obscure your view of the too-recent mound of dirt in the corner that has made you think of certain things in police reports.

But you insist.

"That is where it is buried," he says.

"What's buried?"

"That's where I buried my love after—" he hesitates.

"After you *killed* her?"

"After I killed *it*."

"I don't understand what you mean."

The author does not look at the pile of earth.

"That is where I buried my first childish love of myself,

my belief that I would never die like other people, and that I wasn't the son of my parents but a son of a king, a king who ruled the whole world."

He breaks off.

"But let's get out of here. We'll go upstairs."

In the living room the author's eye is immediately caught by a scene outside the window. The visitor looks—he sees some children playing football on the lawn next door.

"There is another reason why I became an author."

"How's that?"

"Well, I used to play football in a school and there was a coach who didn't like me for a damn. Well, our school was going to play a game up on the Hudson, and I had been substituting for our climax runner who had been hurt the week before. I had a good day substituting for him so now that he was well and had taken his old place I was moved into what might be called the position of blocking back. I wasn't adapted to it, perhaps because there was less glory and less stimulation. It was cold, too, and I don't stand cold, so instead of doing my job I got thinking how grey the skies were. When the coach took me out of the game he said briefly:

"'We simply can't depend on you.'

"I could only answer 'Yes, sir.'

"That was as far as I could explain to him literally what happened—and it's taken me years to figure it out for my own benefit. I had been playing listlessly. We had the other team licked by a couple of touchdowns, and it suddenly occurred to me that I might as well let the opposing end—who hadn't so far made a single tackle—catch a forward pass, but at the last moment I came to life and realized that I couldn't let him catch the pass, but that at least I wouldn't intercept it, so I just knocked it down.

"That was the point where I was taken out of the

game. I remember the desolate ride in the bus back to the train and the desolate ride back to school with everybody thinking I had been yellow on the occasion, when actually I was just distracted and sorry for that opposing end. That's the truth. I've been afraid plenty of times but that wasn't one of the times. The point is it inspired me to write a poem for the school paper which made me as big a hit with my father as if I had become a football hero. So when I went home that Christmas vacation it was in my mind that if you weren't able to function in action you might at least be able to tell about it, because you felt the same intensity—it was a back-door way out of facing reality."

They go into a dining room now. The author walks through it in haste and a certain aversion.

"Don't you enjoy food?" the visitor asks.

"Food—yes! But not the miserable mixture of fruit juices and milk and whole-wheat bread I live on now."

"Are you dyspeptic?"

"Dyspeptic! I'm simply ruined."

"How so?"

"Well, in the Middle West in those days children started life with fried food and waffles and that led into endless malted milks and bacon buns in college and then a little later I jumped to meals at Foyots and the Castello dei Cesari and the Escargot and every spice merchant in France and Italy. And under the name of alcohol— Clarets and Burgundys, Château d'Yquems and Champagnes, Pilsener and Dago Red, prohibition Scotch and Alabama white mule. It was very good while it lasted but I didn't see what pap lay at the end." He shivered. "Let's forget it—it isn't dinner time. Now this—" he says opening a door, "is my study."

A secretary is typing there or rather in a little alcove

adjoining. As they come in she hands the author some letters. His eye falls on the envelope of the first one, his face takes on an expectant smile and he says to the visitor:

"This is the sequel to something that was rather funny. Let me tell you the first part before I open this. Well, about two weeks ago I got a letter under cover from the 'Saturday Evening Post,' addressed not to me but to

Thomas Kracklin,
    Saturday Evening post
        Philadelphia pennsylvania Pa.

On the envelope were several notations evidently by the 'Post's' mail department.

Not known here
Try a story series in 1930 files
Think this is character in story by X in 1927 files.

"This last person had guessed it for Thomas Kracklin was indeed a character in some stories of mine. Here's what the letter said:

Mr. Kracklin I wonder if you are any kin to mine because my name was Kracklin an I had a brother an he did not see us much any more we was worried about him an I thought when I read your story that you was that Kracklin an I thought if I wrote you I would find out yours truly Mrs. Kracklin Lee.

"The address was a small town in Michigan. The letter amused me and was so different from any that I had received for a long time that I made up an answer to it. It went something like this:

My dear Mrs. Kracklin Lee:

I am indeed your long lost brother. I am now in the Baltimore Penitentiary awaiting execution by hanging. If I get out I will be glad to come to visit you. I think you would find me all right except I cannot be irritated as I sometimes kill people if the coffee is cold. But I think I won't be much trouble except for that but I will be pretty poor when I get out of the penitentiary and will be glad if you can take care of me—unless they string me up next Thursday. Write me care of my lawyer.

"Here I gave my name and then signed the letter 'Sincerely, Thomas Kracklin.' This is undoubtedly the answer."

The author opened the envelope—there were two letters inside. The first was addressed to him by his real name.

Dear Sir I hope my brother has not been hung an I thank you for sending his letter I am a poor woman an have no potatoes this day an can just buy the stamp but I hope my brother has not been hung an if not I would like to see him an will you give him this letter yours truly Mrs. Kracklin Lee.

This was the second letter:

Dear Brother I have not got much but if you get off you can come back here an I could not promise to suply you with much but maybe we could get along cannot really promise anythin but I hope you will get off an wish you the very best always your sister Mrs. Kracklin Lee.

When he had finished reading the author said:
"Now isn't it fun to be so damn smart! Miss Palmer,

please write a letter saying her brother's been reprieved and gone to China and put five dollars in the envelope.

"But it's too late," he continued as he and his visitor went upstairs. "You can pay a little money but what can you do for meddling with a human heart? A writer's temperament is continually making him do things he can never repair.

"This is my bedroom. I write a good deal lying down and when there are too many children around, but in summer it's hot up here in the daytime and my hand sticks to the paper."

The visitor moved a fold of cloth to perch himself on the side of a chair but the author warned him quickly:

"Don't touch that! It's just the way somebody left it."

"Oh I beg your pardon."

"Oh it's all right—it was a long long time ago. Sit here for a moment and rest yourself and then we'll go on up."

"Up?"

"Up to the attic. This is a big house you see—on the old-fashioned side."

The attic was the attic of Victorian fiction. It was pleasant, with beams of late light slanting in on piles and piles of magazines and pamphlets and children's school books and college year books and "little" magazines from Paris and ballet programmes and the old "Dial" and "Mercury" and "L'illustration" unbound and the "St. Nicholas" and the journal of the Maryland Historical Society, and piles of maps and guide books from the Golden Gate to Bou Saada. There were files bulging with letters, one marked "letters from my grandfather to my grandmother" and several dozen scrap books and clipping books and photograph books and albums and "baby books" and great envelopes full of unfiled items. . . .

"This is the loot," the author said grimly. "This is what one has instead of a bank balance."

"Are you satisfied?"

"No. But it's nice here sometimes in the late afternoon. This is a sort of a library in its way, you see—the library of a life. And nothing is as depressing as a library if you stay long in it. Unless of course you stay there all the time because then you adjust yourself and become a little crazy. Part of you gets dead. Come on, let's go up."

"Where?"

"Up to the cupola—the turret, the watch-tower, whatever you want to call it. I'll lead the way."

It is small up there and full of baked silent heat until the author opens two of the glass sides that surround it and the twilight wind blows through. As far as your eye can see there is a river winding between green lawns and trees and purple buildings and red slums blended in by a merciful dusk. Even as they stand there the wind increases until it is a gale whistling around the tower and blowing birds past them.

"I lived up here once," the author said after a moment.

"Here? For a long time?"

"No. For just a little while when I was young."

"It must have been rather cramped."

"I didn't notice it."

"Would you like to try it again?"

"No. And I couldn't if I wanted to."

He shivered slightly and closed the windows. As they went downstairs the visitor said, half apologetically: "It's really just like all houses, isn't it?"

The author nodded.

"I didn't think it was when I built it, but in the end I suppose it's just like other houses after all."

—*Esquire*, July 1936

Afternoon of an Author

I

When he woke up he felt better than he had for many weeks, a fact that became plain to him negatively—he did not feel ill. He leaned for a moment against the door frame between his bedroom and bath till he could be sure he was not dizzy. Not a bit, not even when he stooped for a slipper under the bed.

It was a bright April morning, he had no idea what time because his clock was long unwound but as he went back through the apartment to the kitchen he saw that his daughter had breakfasted and departed and that the mail was in, so it was after nine.

"I think I'll go out today," he said to the maid.

"Do you good—it's a lovely day." She was from New Orleans, with the features and coloring of an Arab.

"I want two eggs like yesterday and toast, orange juice and tea."

He lingered for a moment in his daughter's end of the apartment and read his mail. It was an annoying mail with nothing cheerful in it—mostly bills and advertisements with the diurnal Oklahoma school boy and his gaping autograph album. Sam Goldwyn might do a ballet picture with Spessivtzewa and might not—it would all have to wait till Mr. Goldwyn got back from Europe when he might have half a dozen new ideas. Paramount wanted a

141

release on a poem that had appeared in one of the author's books, as they didn't know whether it was an original or quoted. Maybe they were going to get a title from it. Anyhow he had no more equity in that property—he had sold the silent rights many years ago and the sound rights last year.

"Never any luck with movies," he said to himself. "Stick to your last, boy."

He looked out the window during breakfast at the students changing classes on the college campus across the way.

"Twenty years ago I was changing classes," he said to the maid. She laughed her debutante's laugh.

"I'll need a check," she said, "if you're going out."

"Oh, I'm not going out yet. I've got two or three hours' work. I meant late this afternoon."

"Going for a drive?"

"I wouldn't drive that old junk—I'd sell it for fifty dollars. I'm going on the top of a bus."

After breakfast he lay down for fifteen minutes. Then he went into the study and began to work.

The problem was a magazine story that had become so thin in the middle that it was about to blow away. The plot was like climbing endless stairs, he had no element of surprise in reserve, and the characters who started so bravely day-before-yesterday couldn't have qualified for a newspaper serial.

"Yes, I certainly need to get out," he thought. "I'd like to drive down the Shenandoah Valley, or go to Norfolk on the boat."

But both of these ideas were impractical—they took time and energy and he had not much of either—what there was must be conserved for work. He went through the manuscript underlining good phrases in red crayon and after tucking these into a file slowly tore up the rest of the story and dropped it in the waste-basket. Then he walked the room and smoked, occasionally talking to himself.

"Wee-l, let's see—"

"Nau-ow, the next thing—would be—"

"Now let's see, now—"

After awhile he sat down thinking:

"I'm just stale—I shouldn't have touched a pencil for two days."

He looked through the heading "Story Ideas" in his notebook until the maid came to tell him his secretary was on the phone—part-time secretary since he had been ill.

"Not a thing," he said. "I just tore up everything I'd written. It wasn't worth a damn. I'm going out this afternoon."

"Good for you. It's a fine day."

"Better come up tomorrow afternoon—there's a lot of mail and bills."

He shaved, and then as a precaution rested five minutes before he dressed. It was exciting to be going out—he hoped the elevator boys wouldn't say they were glad to see him up and he decided to go down the back elevator where they did not know him. He put on his best suit with the coat and trousers that didn't match. He had bought only two suits in six years but they were the very best suits—the coat alone of this one had cost a hundred and ten dollars. As he must have a destination—it wasn't good to go places without a destination—he put a tube of shampoo ointment in his pocket for his barber to use, and also a small phial of luminol.

"The perfect neurotic," he said, regarding himself in the mirror. "By-product of an idea, slag of a dream."

II

He went into the kitchen and said good-bye to the maid as if he were going to Little America. Once in the war he had commandeered an engine on sheer bluff and had it driven from New York to Washington to keep from being A.W.O.L. Now he stood carefully on the street corner waiting for the light to change, while young people hurried past him with a fine disregard for traffic. On the bus corner under the trees it was green and cool and he thought of Stonewall Jackson's last words: "Let us cross over the river and rest under the shade of the trees." Those Civil War leaders seemed to have realized very suddenly how tired they were—Lee shrivelling into another man, Grant with his desperate memoir-writing at the end.

The bus was all he expected—only one other man on the roof and the green branches ticking against each window through whole blocks. They would probably have to trim those branches and it seemed a pity. There was so much to look at—he tried to define the color of one line of houses and could only think of an old opera cloak of his mother's that was full of tints and yet was of no tint— a mere reflector of light. Somewhere church bells were playing *Venite Adoremus* and he wondered why, because Christmas was eight months off. He didn't like bells but it had been very moving when they played "Maryland, My Maryland" at the governor's funeral.

On the college football field men were working with rollers and a title occurred to him: "Turf-keeper" or else "The Grass Grows," something about a man working on turf for years and bringing up his son to go to college and play football there. Then the son dying in youth and the man's going to work in the cemetery and putting turf over his son instead of under his feet. It would be the kind of piece that is often placed in anthologies, but not his sort of thing—it was sheer swollen antithesis, as formalized as a popular magazine story and easier to write. Many people, however, would consider it excellent because it was melancholy, had digging in it and was simple to understand.

The bus went past a pale Athenian railroad station brought to life by the blue-shirted red-caps out in front. The street narrowed as the business section began and there were suddenly brightly dressed girls, all very beautiful—he thought he had never seen such beautiful girls. There were men too but they all looked rather silly, like himself in the mirror, and there were old undecorative women, and presently, too, there were plain and unpleasant faces among the girls; but in general they were lovely, dressed in real colors all the way from six to thirty, no plans or struggles in their faces, only a state of sweet suspension, provocative and serene. He loved life terribly for a minute, not wanting to give it up at all. He thought perhaps he had made a mistake in coming out so soon.

He got off the bus, holding carefully to all the railings and walked a block to the hotel barbershop. He passed a sporting goods store and looked in the window unmoved except by a first baseman's glove which was already dark in the pocket. Next to that was a haberdasher's and here he stood for quite awhile looking at the deep shade of shirts and the ones of checker and plaid. Ten years ago on the summer Riviera the author and some others had bought dark blue workmen's shirts, and probably that had started that style. The checkered shirts were nice looking, bright as uniforms and he wished he were twenty and going to a beach club all dolled up like a Turner sunset or Guido Reni's dawn.

The barbershop was large, shining and scented—it had

been several months since the author had come down-town on such a mission and he found that his familiar barber was laid up with arthritis; however, he explained to another man how to use the ointment, refused a news-paper and sat, rather happy and sensually content at the strong fingers on his scalp, while a pleasant mingled memory of all the barbershops he had ever known flowed through his mind.

Once he had written a story about a barber. Back in 1929 the proprietor of his favorite shop in the city where he was then living had made a fortune of $300,000 on tips from a local industrialist and was about to retire. The author had no stake in the market, in fact, was about to sail to Europe for a few years with such accumulation as he had, and that autumn hearing how the barber had lost all his fortune he was prompted to write a story, thor-oughly disguised in every way yet hinging on the fact of a barber rising in the world and then tumbling; he heard, nevertheless, that the story had been identified in the city and caused some hard feelings.

The shampoo ended. When he came out into the hall an orchestra had started to play in the cocktail room across the way and he stood for a moment in the door listening. So long since he had danced, perhaps two eve-nings in five years, yet a review of his last book had men-tioned him as being fond of night clubs; the same review had also spoken of him as being indefatigable. Some-thing in the sound of the word in his mind broke him momentarily and feeling tears of weakness behind his eyes he turned away. It was like in the beginning fifteen years ago when they said he had "fatal facility," and he labored like a slave over every sentence so as not to be like that.

"I'm getting bitter again," he said to himself. "That's no good, no good—I've got to go home."

The bus was a long time coming but he didn't like taxis and he still hoped that something would occur to him on that upper-deck passing through the green leaves of the boulevard. When it came finally he had some trouble climbing the steps but it was worth it for the first thing he saw was a pair of high school kids, a boy and a girl, sitting without any self-consciousness on the high pedestal of the Lafayette statue, their attention fast upon each other. Their isolation moved him and he knew he would get something out of it professionally, if only in contrast to the growing seclusion of his life and the increasing necessity of picking over an already well-picked past. He needed re-forestation and he was well aware of it, and he hoped the soil would stand one more growth. It had never been the very best soil for he had had an early weakness for showing off instead of listening and observing.

Here was the apartment house—he glanced up at his own windows on the top floor before he went in.

"The residence of the successful writer," he said to himself. "I wonder what marvelous books he's tearing off up there. It must be great to have a gift like that—just sit down with pencil and paper. Work when you want—go where you please."

His child wasn't home yet but the maid came out of the kitchen and said:

"Did you have a nice time?"

"Perfect," he said. "I went roller-skating and bowled and played around with Man Mountain Dean and finished up in a Turkish Bath. Any telegrams?"

"Not a thing."

"Bring me a glass of milk, will you?"

He went through the dining room and turned into his study, struck blind for a moment with the glow of his two thousand books in the late sunshine. He was quite tired—he would lie down for ten minutes and then see if he could get started on an idea in the two hours before dinner.

—*Esquire*, **August 1936**

An Author's Mother

She was a halting old lady in a black silk dress and a rather preposterously high-crowned hat that some milliner had foisted upon her declining sight. She was downtown with a purpose; she only shopped once a week now and always tried to do a lot in one morning. The doctor had told her she could have the cataracts removed from her eyes but she was over eighty and the thought of the operation frightened her.

Her chief purpose this morning was to buy one of her sons a birthday present. She had intended to get him a bathrobe but passing through the book department of the store and stopping "to see if there was anything new," she saw a big volume on Niaco where she knew he intended to spend the winter—and she turned its pages wondering if he wouldn't like that instead, or if perhaps he already had it.

Her son was a successful author. She had by no means abetted him in the choice of that profession but had wanted him to be an army officer or else go into business like his brother. An author was something distinctly peculiar—there had been only one in the Middle Western city where she was born and he had been regarded as a freak. Of course if her son could have been an author like Longfellow, or Alice and Phoebe Cary, that would have been different, but she did not even remember the names of who wrote the three hundred novels and memoirs that she skimmed through every year. Of course she remembered Mrs. Humphry Ward and now she liked Edna Ferber, but as she lingered in the bookstore this morning her mind kept reverting persistently to the poems of Alice and Phoebe Cary. How lovely the poems had been! Especially the one about the girl instructing the artist how to paint a picture of her mother. Her own mother used to read her that poem.

But the books by her son were not vivid to her, and while she was proud of him in a way, and was always glad when a librarian mentioned him or when someone asked her if she was his mother, her secret opinion was that such a profession was risky and eccentric.

It was a hot morning and feeling suddenly a little faint after her shopping, she told the clerk she would like to sit down for a moment. He got her a chair politely and, as if to reward him by giving him business, she heard herself asking:

"Have you got the poems of Alice and Phoebe Cary?"

He repeated the names.

"Let me see. No—I don't believe we have. I was just looking over the poetry shelves yesterday. We try to keep a few volumes of all the modern poets in stock."

She smiled to herself at his ignorance.

"These poets have been dead many years," she said.

"I don't believe I know of them—but I might be able to order them for you."

"No—never mind."

He seemed an obliging young man and she tried to focus her eyes upon him, for she liked polite young men, but the stacks of books were blurring up a little and she thought she had better go back to her apartment and perhaps order a bathrobe for her son over the telephone.

It was just at the entrance of the store that she fell. There were a few minutes when she was just barely conscious of an annoying confusion centering around her, and then she became gradually aware that she was lying on a sort of bed in what seemed to be an automobile.

The man in white who rode with her spoke to her gently:

"How do you feel now?"

"Oh, I'm all right. Are you taking me home?"

"No, we're taking you to the hospital, Mrs. Johnston—we want to put a little dressing on your forehead. I took the liberty of looking in your shopping bag and finding out your name. Will you tell me the name and address of your nearest relatives?"

Once again consciousness began to slip away and she spoke vaguely of her son who was a business man in the West and of a granddaughter who had just opened a millinery shop in Chicago. But before he could get anything definite she dismissed the subject as if it were irrelevant and made an effort to rise from the stretcher.

"I want to go home. I don't know why you're taking me to a hospital—I've never been in a hospital."

"You see, Mrs. Johnston, you came out of a store and tripped and fell down some stairs, and unfortunately you have a cut."

"My son will write about it."

"What!" asked the interne rather surprised.

The old woman repeated vaguely: "My son will write about it."

"Is your son in the journalistic business?"

"Yes—but you mustn't let him know. You mustn't disturb—"

"Don't talk for just a moment, Mrs. Johnston—I want to keep this little cut together till we can make a suture."

Nonetheless she moved her head and said in a determined voice:

"I didn't say my son was a suture—I said he was an author."

"You misunderstood me, Mrs. Johnston. I meant about your forehead. A 'suture' is where someone cuts themselves a little—"

Her pulse fluttered and he gave her spirits of ammonia to hold her till she got to the hospital door.

"No, my son is not a suture," she said. "Why did you say that? He's an *au*thor." She spoke very slowly as if she was unfamiliar with the words coming from her tired mouth. "An author is someone who writes books."

They had reached the hospital and the interne was busy trying to disembark her from the ambulance. "—Yes, I understand, Mrs. Johnston. Now try and keep your head quite still."

"My apartment is three-o-five," she said.

"We just want you to come into the hospital a few hours. What sort of books does your son write, Mrs. Johnston?"

"Oh he writes all sorts of books."

"Just try to hold your head still, Mrs. Johnston. What name does your son write under?"

"Hamilton T. Johnston. But he's an author not a suture. Are you a suture?"

"No, Mrs. Johnston, I'm a doctor."

"Well, this doesn't look like my apartment." In one gesture she pulled what was left of her together and said: "Well, don't disturb my son John or my son-in-law or my daughter that died or my son Hamilton who—" She raised herself to a supreme effort and remembering the only book she knew really in her heart announced astonishingly, "—my son, Hamilton, who wrote 'The Poems of Alice and Phoebe Cary—'" Her voice was getting weaker and as they carried the stretcher into the elevator her pulse grew feebler and feebler and the interne knew there would not be any suture, that nature had put its last stitch in that old forehead. But he could not know what she was thinking at the last, and would never have guessed it was that Alice and Phoebe Cary had come to call upon her, and taken her hands, and led her back gently into the country she understood.

—*Esquire*, September 1936

My Generation

In 1918 the present writer stole an engine, together with its trustful engineer, and drove two hundred miles in it to keep from being A.W.O.L. He can still be tried for the offense, so the details must remain undisclosed. It is set down here only to bear witness to the fact that in those days we were red-blooded—*Children! Don't bring those parachutes into the house!* All right—we'll drop that approach altogether.

We who are now between forty and forty-five were born mostly at home in gas-light or in the country by oil lamps. Mewling and burping unscientifically in our nurses' arms we were unaware of being the Great Inheritors—unaware that, as we took over the remnants of the crumbled Spanish Empire, the robe of primacy was being wrapped around our little shoulders. About ten million of us were born with the Empire, and in our first Buster Brown collars we were treated to a new kind of circus parade, a Wild West show on water—the Fleet was being sent on a trip to show the world. At the turn of the previous century—in 1800—it had likewise been bracing to be an American, but that was from ignorance, for beyond our own shore we were a small potato indeed. This time, though, there was no doubt of it—when even our nursery books showed the last sinking turrets of Cervera's fleet we were incorrigibly a great nation.

We were the great believers. Edmund Wilson has remarked that the force of the disillusion in "A Farewell to Arms" derives from Hemingway's original hope and belief. Without that he could not have written of the war: "finally only the names of places had dignity. . . . Abstract words such as glory, honor, courage, or hallow were obscene beside the concrete names of villages, the numbers of roads, the names of rivers, the numbers of regiments and the dates." Hemingway felt that way in 1918. In 1899 when he was born there was faith and hope such as few modern nations have known.

It is important just when a generation first sees the light—and by a generation I mean that reaction against the fathers which seems to occur about three times in a century. It is distinguished by a set of ideas, inherited in moderated form from the madmen and the outlaws of the generation before; if it is a real generation it has its own leaders and spokesmen, and it draws into its orbit those born just before it and just after, whose ideas are less clear-cut and defiant. A strongly individual generation sprouts most readily from a time of stress and emergency—tensity, communicated from parent to child, seems to leave a pattern on the heart. The generation which reached maturity around 1800 was born spiritually at Valley Forge. Its milk was the illiterate letters, the verbal messages, the casualty reports written during the desperate seven-year retreat from Massachusetts to the Carolinas—and the return back to the Virginia town; its toys were the flintlock in the corner, the epaulettes of a Hessian grenadier; its first legend the print of Washington on the schoolroom wall. It grew up to be the hardboiled generation of Andrew Jackson and Daniel Webster, Fulton and Eli Whitney, Lewis and Clark. Its few authors, Washington Irving and Cooper, struggled to give America a past, a breathing record of those who had known its forests and fields and towns, a special service for its dead.

They were tougher and rougher than their fathers; they were adrift in a land more remote from the mainstream and all their doubt clothed them in desperation. They revived the duel, long moribund in England. They had a mess on their hands—Washington had died with more apprehension for the republic than he had felt at the lowest ebb of the revolution, and the forces of the time gave life a restless stamp. In retrospect the men seem all of one piece. When the last of them, old General Winfield Scott, watched a new tragedy begin at Bull Run there could have been few men alive to whom he could speak the language of his broken heart.

In haste let me add that my generation is very much alive. One of us recently married Hedy Lamarr!

II

We were born to power and intense nationalism. We did not have to stand up in a movie house and recite a child's pledge to the flag to be aware of it. We were told, individually and as a unit, that we were a race that could potentially lick ten others of any genus. This is not a nostalgic article for it has a point to make—but we began life in post-Fauntleroy suits (often a sailor's uniform as a taunt to Spain). Jingo was the lingo—we saw plays named "Paul Revere" and "Secret Service" and raced toy boats called the *Columbia* and the *Reliance* after the cup defenders. We carved our own swords whistling "Way Down in Colon Town," where we would presently engage in battle with lesser breeds. We sang "Tease Me, Coax Me, Kiss Me Good Night," "Dear Love," and "If You Talk in Your

Sleep Don't Mention My Name" (which, due to the malice of some false friends, was Fitzboomski all through the Russo-Japanese war). We made "buck-boards" out of velocipede wheels and didn't get a page in "Life" about it, and we printed our own photographs in fading brown and blue. The mechanical age was coming fast but many of the things we played with we made ourselves.

That America passed away somewhere between 1910 and 1920; and the fact gives my generation its uniqueness—we are at once pre-war and post-war. We were well grown in the tense spring of 1917, but for the most part not married and settled. The peace found us almost intact—less than five percent of my college class were killed in the war, and the colleges had a high average compared to the country as a whole. Men of our age in Europe simply do not exist. I have looked for them often, but they are twenty-five years dead.

So we inherited two worlds—the one of hope to which we had been bred; the one of disillusion which we had discovered early for ourselves. And that first world was growing as remote as another country, however close in time. My father wrote the old-fashioned ∫ for "s" in his youthful letters and as a boy during the Civil War was an integral part of the Confederate spy system between Washington and Richmond. In moments of supreme exasperation he said, "Confound it!" I live without madness in a world of scientific miracles where curses or Promethean cries are bolder—and more ineffectual. I do not "accept" that world, as for instance my daughter does. But I function in it with familiarity, and to a growing extent my generation are beginning to run it.

III

What are these men who, about the time of their majority, found themselves singing "We're in the army now." Their first discovery of 1919 was that nobody cared. Cut out the war talk—every so often life was doomed to be a cock-eyed and disorderly business. Forget quickly.

All right then. Hack McGraw, who had been a major in France, came back to Princeton and captained a winning football team—I never saw him play without wondering what he thought about it all. Tommy Hitchcock, who had escaped from Germany by jumping from a train, went up to Harvard—perhaps to find out why. The best musician I ever knew was so confused that he walked out to put shirts on girls in the Society Islands! Men of fifty had the gall to tell us that when their cellars were exhausted they would drink no more—but they had fixed it so *we* could start with rot-gut right now. Most of us took a drink by that time but honestly it wasn't our invention—though both moonshine and heavy necking, which had spread up from the Deep South and out of Chicago as early as 1915, were put upon our bill.

The truth was that we found the youth younger than ourselves, the sheiks and the flappers, rather disturbing. We had settled down to work. George Gershwin was picking out tunes between other peoples' auditions in Tin Pan Alley and Ernest Hemingway was reporting the massacres in Smyrna. Ben Hecht and Charlie MacArthur were watching the Chicago underworld in bud. Dempsey, scarred in reverse by the war, was becoming the bravo of his day, while Tunney bided his time. Donald Peattie was coming into his inheritance of the woods and what he found there. George Antheil's music and Paul Nelson's suspended house were a little way off, but Vincent Youmans already had charmed his audience with "Oh Me, Oh My, Oh You." Merian Cooper would fly a little longer as a soldier of fortune before settling down to make "Chang" and "Grass." Denny Holden wasn't through with war either—in his plane last summer perished a gallant and lively jack-of-many-trades whose life was a hundred stories.

The late Tom Wolfe left the Norfolk ship-yards and went to college for more education. His end was so tragic that I am glad I knew him in care-free and fortunate times. He had that flair for the extravagant and fantastic which has been an American characteristic from Irving and Poe to Dashiell Hammett. He was six feet eight inches tall and I was with him one night on Lake Geneva when he found to his amazement that not only could he reach the street wires over his head but that when he pulled them he caused a blackout of Montreux. To the inquiring mind this is something of a discovery, not a thing that happens every day. I had a hard time getting Tom away from there quickly. Windows opened, voices called, there were running footsteps, and still Tom played at his blackout with the casualness of a conductor ringing up fares. We drove over the French border that night.

Wolfe was a grievous loss. With Hemingway, Dos Passos, Wilder and Faulkner he was one of a group of talents for fiction such as rarely appear in a single hatching. Each of these authors created a world quite his own and lived in it convincingly. Decimated Europe had nothing to set beside the work of these young men.

The poets of my time set a more precarious course, or so I believe, for the novel had become elastic enough to say almost anything. But some of the critics, Wilson, Mumford, Seldes among others, have had powerful influence upon the taste and interests of the past two decades. The playwrights, Sherwood and Behrman, Barry and

Stallings, Hecht and MacArthur, have been so successful that they are now their own angels. Contemplating a
production they call for the private sucker list—and find
their own names at the top. And that art which stock-
holders, producers and public have kept in its perennial
infancy owes a great debt to those two directors, Frank
Capra and King Vidor, who have fought themselves free
of producers' control.

All in all it was a husky generation. Match me Tommy
Hitchcock or Bill Tilden for sheer power of survival as
champions. Outside of a few eastern cities there was
a vacant lot in every block and I played humbly on the
same teams with future Minnesota linemen, a national
golf medalist, Dudley Mudge, and a national amateur
champion, Harrison Johnston.

Later, pursued from hideout to hideout by the truant
officers, I came in early contact with a few incipient men
of letters. I was at prep school in New Jersey with Pulitzer Prizeman Herbert Agar and novelists Cyril Hume
and Edward Hope (Coffey). Hope and I were destined
to follow a similar pattern—to write librettos at Princeton, "drool" for the college comic and, later, college novels. But I remember him best when he was center and I
was quarterback on the second team at school. We were
both fifteen—and awful. There were a couple of 180-
pound tackles (one of them now headmaster for his sins)
who liked to practice taking me out, and Hope gave me
no protection—no protection at all—and I would have
paid well for protection. We were the laziest and lowest-
ranking boys in school.

In college I was luckier. I knew the future presidents
of many banks and oil companies, the governor of Tennessee, and among the intellectuals encountered John
Peale Bishop, War-Bird Elliott Springs, Judge John Biggs
and Hamilton Fish Armstrong. Of course I had no idea

who they were, and neither did they, or I could have started an autographed tablecloth. Things were stirring: Richard Cleveland, Henry Strater and David Bruce led a revolt against the "social system." Spence Pumpelly and Charlie Taft did the same at Yale.

Next on my list I find Al Capone, born in 1899—but he saw the light in Naples. Anyhow it's a good place to stop.

IV

Those I have mentioned are only a platoon in an army of five million. Are they representative of my generation—of those who have one foot planted before the war and one after it? They are at any rate the articulate and my claim is that they have not been "sheltered"—when any moppet assures me that we "lived in an Ivory Tower," my blood boils and I weep into my paraldehyde. "The Jungle" and "The Octopus" were on our shelves before John Steinbeck ate the grape of wrath. In 1920 the present writer recommended the immediate machine-gunning of all men in a position to marry. The revolution wasn't just around the corner—it was under my hat. But it is a fact that the capacity of this generation to believe has run very thin. The war, the peace, the boom, the depression, the shadow of the new war scarcely correspond to the idea of manifest destiny. Many men of my age are inclined to paraphrase Sir Edward Grey of 1914—"The lamps are going out all over the world—we shall not see them lit again in our time."

It should be said that Steinbeck and Dr. Hutchins, Peter Arno and the late Irving Thalberg, Caldwell and O'Hara, Saroyan and Odets, Colonel Lindbergh and District Attorney Dewey were all too young to play on our team. Their experiences, achievements, and certainties are not of our world. We are closer in time to the hulk in a veterans' hospital—for these younger men did not dance the Grizzly Bear and the Bunny Hug when one was risking ostracism, or march a thousand miles to "Beautiful Katy." But they swim, one and all, in our orbit; as the painter Picasso says: "You do something *first* and then somebody comes along and does it pretty." *Easy with that Space gun! You oughtn't to point things!* By and large I grant them a grace we do not have, and for all we know the Messiah may be among them. But we are something else again.

Well—many are dead, and some I have quarreled with and don't see any more. But I have never cared for any men as much as for these who felt the first springs when I did, and saw death ahead, and were reprieved—and who now walk the long stormy summer. It is a generation staunch by inheritance, sophisticated by fact—and rather deeply wise. More than that, what I feel about them is summed up in a line of Willa Cather's: "We possess together the precious, the incommunicable past."

—Composed and revised in 1939–1940;
first published in *Esquire*, October 1968

Annotations

Fitzgerald's writings are filled with references to politicians, stage performers, screen stars, athletes, military heroes, night clubs, hotels, restaurants, literary works, styles of dance, popular songs, and much more—all familiar to his readers in the 1920s and 1930s but unknown to us today. The identifications and annotations below will help to place Fitzgerald's essays in the context of his times. The annotations are keyed to the text by page number.

Page 1: **"The Quaker Girl"** This British musical comedy opened in New York in October 1911. The title character, played by Ina Claire, wins the heart of a young American who is visiting an English town.

Page 1: **"His Honor the Sultan"** . . . **Triangle Club of Princeton** The Triangle Club, founded at Princeton in 1891, was a student musical-comedy group that took its productions on tour during the Christmas holidays. Undergraduate boys played all of the parts, including the female roles—hence much of the humor in the productions, which always included a dance number with a kick-line. Fitzgerald wrote the lyrics for three Triangle scripts during his years at Princeton. Triangle shows invariably had preposterous plots: the story line for *His Honor the Sultan*, for example, involves an attempt to dethrone Sultan Murad VI of Tanjocco and put in his place Herr Heinrich Schlitz, a correspondent for the German newspaper *Die Fliegende Blätter*.

Page 2: **Rupert Brooke** This English poet was one of Fitzgerald's early literary heroes. Brooke's death from septicemia during the First

World War made him an iconic figure for many young writers. Fitzgerald took the title of his first novel, *This Side of Paradise* (1920), from Brooke's poem "Tiare Tahiti."

Page 3: **"The Romantic Egotist"** Fitzgerald incorporated much material from this rejected novel into Book I of *This Side of Paradise*. He changed the hero's name from Stephen Palms to Amory Blaine and recast the story from first-person to third-person narration.

Page 4: **"That's all there is; there isn't any more."** Spoken not by Julius Caesar but by the American actress Ethel Barrymore at the conclusion of each of her performances.

"AN INTERVIEW WITH MR. FITZGERALD"

Page 5: **the Biltmore** The Fitzgeralds began their honeymoon (which coincided with the publication of *This Side of Paradise*) at the Biltmore Hotel, a large, elegant establishment at Madison and 43rd, just across from Grand Central Terminal. Because their carousing disturbed the other guests, they were asked to leave; they moved to the Commodore, nearby at 42nd and Lexington.

Page 6: *The Ring and the Book* Robert Browning's long poem *The Ring and the Book* (1868–69) is a re-creation of a seventeenth-century murder trial in Italy. Many critics consider it to be his greatest achievement.

Page 7: **Hichens** Of the authors mentioned in this paragraph, only the prolific Robert Smythe Hichens, a popular *fin-de-siècle* aesthete, has fallen from the canon. He is remembered today for his ornate style, on display in his best-known novel, *The Green Carnation* (1894).

"THREE CITIES"

Page 8: **Dreiser's suppressed "Genius"** Theodore Dreiser's controversial novel *The "Genius"* (1915) was withdrawn from American sale by its publisher, John Lane Co., under pressure from public moralists. Fitzgerald would have had difficulty purchasing a copy in the U.S. but was able to acquire a copy with relative ease in Paris. Dreiser's *The Titan* (1914) is the second novel in his Trilogy of Desire; the other two volumes are *The Financier* (1912) and *The Stoic* (1947).

Page 9: *Carabinieri* . . . *Bersaglieri* The *Carabinieri* are the national police of Italy; the *Bersaglieri* are a corps of light infantry in the Italian army.

Page 9: **John Carter . . . "These Wild Young People"** John F. Carter, Jr., caused a stir by publishing "'These Wild Young People,' by One of Them" in the September 1920 issue of the *Atlantic Monthly*. The article, about the fast, extravagant youths of Fitzgerald's generation, was mentioned in several reviews of Fitzgerald's debut novel, *This Side of Paradise* (1920).

Page 9: **"Alice Adams" . . . "Moon-Calf"** The novelist Booth Tarkington, like Fitzgerald an alumnus of Princeton, was one of the most successful professional authors of the period. Among his books are *The Magnificent Ambersons* (1918), *Ramsey Milholland* (1919), and *Alice Adams* (1921). Floyd Dell's coming-of-age novel *Moon-Calf* (1920) was compared to *This Side of Paradise* by several New York book critics.

Page 10: **"Sinister Street," "Zuleika Dobson" and "Jude the Obscure"** Three novels by British writers whom Fitzgerald admired. Compton Mackenzie's *Sinister Street* (1914) had a strong influence on *This Side of Paradise*; Max Beerbohm's *Zuleika Dobson* (1911) is a comic fantasy; *Jude the Obscure* (1896) was Thomas Hardy's last novel.

Page 10: **The High . . . Via Appia** High Street, one of the major thoroughfares in Oxford, is known to residents of the city as "The High." The Via Appia, or Appian Way, was one of the most important roads of the ancient Roman republic.

"WHAT I THINK AND FEEL AT 25"

Page 14: **Eighteenth Amendment** Prohibition was instituted by the Eighteenth Amendment to the U.S. Constitution; the measure went into effect on January 16, 1919, and was enforced by the Volstead Act.

Page 15: **Rockefeller Institute** This institute for medical research, which included laboratories and a hospital, was founded in New York City in 1901 by the American industrialist John D. Rockefeller.

Page 15: **Zion City** The city of Zion, Illinois, was established in 1901 by John Alexander Dowie, the founder of the Christian Catholic Church. Initially he governed Zion himself; he was deposed in 1905, but Zion maintained a theocratic government until 1935.

Page 20: **munching a loaf of bread** An allusion to a passage in *The Autobiography of Benjamin Franklin* in which Franklin, newly arrived in Philadelphia, purchases "three great Puffy Rolls" at a bakery and walks about the streets "with a Roll under each Arm, and eating the other."

Page 23: **an article . . . by a fellow named Ring Lardner** Fitzgerald has in mind Lardner's "General Symptoms of Being 35—Which Is What I Am," from the May 1921 issue of *American Magazine*.

"IMAGINATION—AND A FEW MOTHERS"

Page 25: **Mother Hubbards** Loose flowing gowns, named for the nursery-rhyme character. Early missionaries tried to persuade Polynesian women to wear them.

Page 26: **as Shelley did *not* put it** Fitzgerald is alluding to Percy Bysshe Shelley's "To ___: One Word Is Too Often Profaned," first published in *Posthumous Poems* (1824). Shelley's lines read "The desire of the moth for the star, / Of the night for the morrow. . . ."

Page 34: **the Hippodrome** This indoor arena, on Sixth Avenue between 43rd and 44th Streets, was famous for its spectacular programs, which often included aquatic feats, elephant acts, and even flying dirigibles.

"HOW TO LIVE ON $36,000 A YEAR"

Page 35: **Liberty Bonds** These government bonds helped to finance American participation in the First World War. They paid 3.5 percent interest and were authorized by the First Liberty Loan Act of 1917.

Page 37: **a town about fifteen miles from New York** This is Great Neck, Long Island, where the Fitzgeralds lived from October 1922 until April 1924. Fitzgerald gathered much of the material for *The Great Gatsby* while living in Great Neck.

Page 38: **a tendency to remove his collar** Men during this period wore shirts with detachable collars that were held to the body of the shirt by studs or collar buttons. It would have been bad manners to remove one's shirt collar at a dinner party.

Page 39: **the gold rush of '49, or a big bonanza of the '70's** Two periods of economic optimism. The discovery of gold in 1848 at Sutter's Mill near Coloma, California, caused the famous California Gold Rush the following year. The post–Civil War financial boom in the U.S. lasted until 1873. The failure in that year of Jay Cooke & Co., a prominent banking house, caused financial panic and prompted the U.S. Treasury to adopt the gold standard.

Page 41: **I had begun a new novel** This was the earliest version of *The Great Gatsby*, begun by Fitzgerald in June 1923. Two pages of this attempt survive among his papers at Princeton; they are narrated in the third person.

Page 42: **the first act of my play** Fitzgerald eventually published the script of *The Vegetable, or from President to Postman*, with Scribner's in April 1923.

Page 44: **Framed crayon portraits** These crayon portraits of Fitzgerald and Zelda by the illustrator James Montgomery Flagg were published with their article "Looking Back Eight Years," in the June 1928 issue of *College Humor*. The portraits are reproduced in *The Romantic Egotists* (New York: Scribner's, 1974), 162–63.

Page 47: **the Dempsey-Firpo fight** On September 14, 1923, heavyweight champion Jack Dempsey successfully defended his title against the Argentinian Luis Firpo at the Polo Grounds in New York City. More than 88,000 spectators attended the fight. Ringside seats would have been expensive.

"HOW TO LIVE ON PRACTICALLY NOTHING A YEAR"

Page 52: **the Wembley exhibition** The British Empire Exhibition of 1924–25 was held at Wembley, near London. The displays emphasized industry and the arts; the first version of Wembley Stadium was constructed for the occasion.

Page 54: **a Rue de la Paix hat** This Paris street is famous for its jewelry stores and women's clothing establishments. The prospective nurse was wearing a stylish, high-priced hat.

Page 55: **Mr. and Mrs. Douglas Fairbanks** The American film stars Douglas Fairbanks and Mary Pickford were married in 1920. He was famous for his swashbuckler roles; she was known as "America's Sweetheart." When not traveling, they lived in Hollywood at their country estate, called Pickfair. The Fitzgeralds visited them there in 1927.

Page 55: **wood-alcohol** One of the attractions of Paris was that one did not have to drink the decoctions of American bootleggers, which might be laced with wood alcohol or lead.

Page 56: **the fairy blue of Maxfield Parrish's pictures** Parrish's illustrations, posters, and murals were popular during the 1920s. He was known for a trademark color called "Parrish blue," mentioned in the final scene of Fitzgerald's novella *May Day* (1920).

Page 60: **"Yes, we have no villas today . . ."** A reference to one of the most popular American songs of the 1920s, "Yes, We Have No Bananas!" by Frank Silver and Irving Cohn.

Page 62: **the Man with the Iron Mask** This French prisoner (probably Count Girolamo Mattioli) was imprisoned for more than forty years by Louis XIV. He was the subject of the romance *L'homme au masque de fer* (1848–50) by the elder Dumas.

Page 64: **the "Illustrated London News"** This international newspaper provided information about British politics and social life. During the First World War, Fitzgerald read its accounts of the fighting in France and Belgium.

Page 65: **Catherine de Medici . . . St. Bartholomew's** Catherine was queen of France during the reign of Henry II. She helped to plan the massacre of St. Bartholomew's Day, an attack on Protestant leaders, which began in Paris on August 24, 1572, and brought about civil war.

Page 71: **white ducks** The young aviators (one of whom was probably Zelda's admirer Edouard Jozan) were wearing uniforms made of white duck, a light cotton or linen cloth.

Page 71: *carmagnole* This lively song and round dance, popular during the French Revolution, was named after Carmagnola, a town in Piedmont occupied by the revolutionaries. The short jacket with wide lapels and metal buttons that they wore was also called a *carmagnole*.

" 'WAIT TILL YOU HAVE CHILDREN OF YOUR OWN!' "

Page 74: **"And I hope she'll be a fool . . ."** Fitzgerald gives these lines to Daisy in Chapter I of *The Great Gatsby*, p. 21 of the Scribner's first edition.

Page 76: **Grover Cleveland Bergdoll's childish treble** Bergdoll dodged the draft during the war, fleeing to Germany to escape conscription. Ironically, the German government tried to force him to enlist in its own military. Bergdoll returned to the U.S. in 1939; he was tried, convicted, and imprisoned until 1946.

Page 77: **Van Loon's "Story of Mankind"** This work of popular history by Hendrik Willem van Loon was a bestseller for the publisher Horace Liveright in 1921.

Page 79: **Pollyanna** The title character of this 1913 novel by Eleanor H. Porter always looks on the bright side and plays the "glad game." Her name became synonymous with fatuous optimism and idealism.

Page 80: **Anthony Hope . . . J. S. Fletcher . . . "Foster's Bridge"** Anthony Hope was the pseudonym of Sir Anthony Hope Hawkins, author of numerous novels and plays, including *The Prisoner of Zenda* (1894). The stories of the British detective novelist Joseph Smith Fletcher were popular during the 1920s and 1930s. Robert Frederick Foster, an authority on card games, published *Foster's Bridge* in 1902.

Page 81: **Ted Coy, the Yale football star . . . a certain obscure Jesuit priest** Ted Coy played football at Yale from 1906 to 1909; the character Ted Fay in Fitzgerald's short story "The Freshest Boy" (1928) is based on Coy. The Jesuit priest is Monsignor Sigourney Fay, Fitzgerald's mentor at the Newman School during his prep years and the dedicatee of *This Side of Paradise*. Ted Fay's last name is taken from Monsignor Fay, thus linking these two men whom Fitzgerald had admired as a boy.

Page 81: **Richard Harding Davis** One of the most popular American authors of the late 1890s, the dashing journalist Richard Harding Davis covered several wars for major newspapers and wrote fiction featuring his character Cortland Van Bibber, a Robin Hood of the upper classes.

Page 81: **Taft . . . John Drew** William Howard Taft and William McKinley were former U.S. presidents. The populist politician William Jennings Bryan ran unsuccessfully three times for the presidency. Nelson Appleton Miles led troops during the Indian wars of the late 1800s. William Rufus Shafter commanded the army that invaded Cuba during the Spanish-American War of 1898. As a commodore during this same war, Winfield Scott Schley oversaw the battle of Santiago. George Dewey, another hero of the Spanish-American War, was mentioned as a presidential candidate in later years. The novelist and editor William Dean Howells was a proponent of realism in American literature. The popular artist Frederic Remington depicted horses, cowboys, Indians, and mounted soldiers in his paintings and sculptures. The industrialist and philanthropist Andrew Carnegie made his fortune in the steel industry. James J. Hill, from Fitzgerald's native St. Paul, built railroads in the upper midwestern and western states. John D. Rockefeller became famous for his philanthropy and infamous for his Standard Oil monopoly. The handsome stage actor John Drew played both dramatic and comedic roles.

Page 81: **Stonewall Jackson . . . General Gordon** The majority of these men died romantic deaths. The Confederate general Thomas J. (Stonewall) Jackson was accidentally killed by one of his own men at Chancellorsville. The Belgian missionary Father Damien died while working in a leper colony on the Hawaiian island of Molokai. George Rogers Clark, an American general during the Revolutionary War, led successful campaigns against the British in the Old Northwest. Major John André, a charming British spy, was captured, tried, and executed by the Americans during the same war. Lord Byron died in Greece in 1824 while attempting to unite Greek rebels against the Ottoman Empire. James Ewell Brown (Jeb) Stuart, a flamboyant Confederate cavalry commander, died in action at the Battle of Yellow Tavern. Giuseppe Garibaldi led military campaigns to unite Italy under Victor Emmanuel II in 1861. Charles Dickens was one of Fitzgerald's favorite authors, perhaps because of his impoverished upbringing. Roger Williams founded Rhode Island as a haven for refugees from religious persecution. Charles George Gordon, a popular British general known as "Chinese Gordon," held out with his forces for ten months during the siege of Khartoum but eventually was killed, two days before help arrived.

Page 81: **Stanford White, E. H. Harriman, and Stephen Crane** The architect Stanford White designed the first Madison Square Garden and the Washington Arch; he was shot to death by Harry K. Thaw in a dispute over Thaw's wife, the actress Evelyn Nesbit. The business practices of Edward Henry Harriman, a railroad executive, were investigated and condemned by the Interstate Commerce Commission in 1907. Stephen Crane was famous for his novels *Maggie: A Girl of the Streets* (1893) and *The Red Badge of Courage* (1895), but his reputation was clouded by his marriage to Cora Taylor, the owner of a Florida brothel, and by his use of drugs and alcohol.

Page 82: **Cummings, Otto Braun, Dos Passos, Wilson, Ferguson, Thomas Boyd** Fitzgerald admired E. E. Cummings' autobiographical book *The Enormous Room* (1922), a prose account of his internment in France during the First World War, and John Dos Passos' war novel *Three Soldiers*. Otto Braun was a young German Jewish soldier; passages from his wartime diary were published in *The Diary of Otto Braun* (1924). The journalist and critic Edmund Wilson, who served in the army during the war, is mentioned in several of the essays in this collection; he was Fitzgerald's friend at Princeton and later became his "intellectual conscience." John Alexander Ferguson wrote a book of wartime poetry called *On Vimy Ridge* (1917). Thomas Boyd, a friend of Fitzgerald's from St. Paul, wrote *Through the Wheat* (1923), a novel about trench warfare on the Western Front.

Page 83: **Lucy Stone League** Lucy Stone was an abolitionist and crusader for women's rights. She founded the *Woman's Journal*, the official magazine of the National American Woman Suffrage Association. After her death her daughter carried on her work through the Lucy Stone League.

"HOW TO WASTE MATERIAL"

Page 86: **Corona** A brand of portable typewriter used by some of Fitzgerald's contemporaries in the writing trade.

Page 86: **Richard Harding Davis and John Fox, Jr.** Both authors reported on the Spanish-American War. Fox, one of the Rough Riders, became a magazine correspondent and later wrote romantic stories about the Cumberland Mountains, including *The Little Shepherd of Kingdom Come* (1903) and *The Trail of the Lonesome Pine* (1908). (Fitzgerald is alluding to these books in the first part of this sentence.) Davis is glossed above in the notes for "Wait Till You Have Children of Your Own!"

Page 87: **H. L. Mencken** Mencken, a prominent journalist, was Fitzgerald's friend and advocate, especially during the early years of his career. Known as H.L.M. and "The Baltimore Sage," he is remembered today for his coverage of the Scopes Monkey Trial of 1925 and for his four-volume work, *The American Language*.

Page 88: **Waldo Frank . . . Hergesheimer** Frank, a novelist and critic, was one of the founders of *The Seven Arts*. His fiction was characterized by mysticism, introspective analysis, and a poeticized style. Joseph Hergesheimer, a successful American novelist during the early years of Fitzgerald's career, is remembered today for *The Three Black Pennys* (1917) and *Cytherea* (1922).

Page 89: **"Les Croix de Bois"** This widely read novel by Roland Dorgelès was based on his experiences in trench warfare. Fitzgerald probably read the English translation, entitled *Wooden Crosses* (1919)—with French slang rendered as British slang, e.g.: "You're never going to drive these poor blighters daft already with your flash patter . . ." (p. 6).

Page 89: **"In Our Time"** Fitzgerald wrote this appreciation to mark the publication, by Boni & Liveright, of Hemingway's first collection of stories, *In Our Time* (1925). Hemingway had earlier published the short "interchapters" in Paris as *in our time* (Three Mountains Press, 1924).

"PRINCETON"

Page 92: **senior societies** The most prestigious of the senior societies at Yale was Skull and Bones. The others, when Fitzgerald wrote this essay, were Scroll and Key, Berzelius, Book and Snake, Wolf's Head, and Elihu.

Page 92: **Jesse Lynch Williams** This alumnus of Princeton caused a stir with accounts of undergraduate drinking in his two books *Princeton Stories* (1895) and *The Adventures of a Freshman* (1899). Later Williams became a successful dramatist; he won a Pulitzer Prize for his play *Why Marry?*

Page 93: **Lee Higginson & Company** This Boston banking firm was headed by Henry Lee Higginson, a Harvard alumnus who was an ardent supporter of the football program. In 1890 he donated the land for Soldiers Field, where football games were played. Fitzgerald is alluding to rumors that Higginson paid Harvard football players under the table.

Page 93: **"Fly" or "Porcellian" . . . Groton or St. Mark's** Two of the oldest and most prestigious of the final social clubs at Harvard. Fitzgerald is suggesting that membership in both clubs depended on whether one had attended the proper prep school.

Page 94: **Two tall spires . . . Gothic architecture . . . Nassau Hall . . . Hessian bullets** Princeton is known for its collegiate Gothic architecture, a style developed by the architect Ralph Adams Cram. The two spires mentioned here are those of Holder Tower on Nassau Street and Cleveland Tower in the Graduate College. Nassau Hall, erected in 1756, is the oldest building at Princeton. Both British and American troops occupied the structure during the Revolutionary War; it was shelled by George Washington's troops and fired upon by Hessian soldiers. A mark left by a cannonball is still visible today on the south wall of the west wing.

Page 94: **Alfred Noyes** This English poet, critic, and essayist, remembered for his ballads and narrative verse, taught English literature at Princeton while Fitzgerald was a student there and edited *A Book of Princeton Verse 1916*, which contains work by Princeton students.

Page 94: **President McCosh** James McCosh, the eleventh president of Princeton, served from 1868 to 1888. He assembled a distinguished faculty, modernized the plan of study, and put into motion an ambitious program of building and expansion.

Page 94: **Booth Tarkington** Tarkington, mentioned above in "Three Cities," was a cofounder of the Triangle Club. He became a popular fiction writer; his "Penrod" stories served as models for Fitzgerald's Basil Duke Lee stories (1928–29).

Page 94: **Wilson's cloistered plans** Woodrow Wilson, thirteenth president of Princeton, introduced a structured program of study and hired some fifty preceptors to function as guides and tutors for the undergraduates. He attempted to replace the eating clubs with a residential quad system but was unsuccessful; he left Princeton in 1910 to run successfully for the governorship of New Jersey and became president of the United States in 1913.

Page 95: **Gertrude Ederle and Mrs. Snyder** The American swimmer Gertrude Ederle was the first woman to swim the English

Channel. Two million people lined the streets to cheer for her when she returned to New York. Ruth Snyder, sentenced to death for the murder of her husband, was the first woman to die in the electric chair in the United States. A reporter from the *New York Daily News* contrived to photograph her just as the switch was thrown.

Page 95: **Johnny Poe with the Black Watch in Flanders** John Prentiss Poe, Jr., was one of six brothers who attended Princeton and played football there. He enlisted in the British army during the First World War and was assigned to the Scottish infantry unit known as the Black Watch, after their dark plaid kilts. Poe was killed in action in France in September 1915.

Page 95: **the romantic Buzz Law** This football hero starred for Princeton during Fitzgerald's freshman year. The play Fitzgerald remembers occurred on November 15, 1913, when Princeton and Yale played to a 3–3 tie in New Haven. Hobey Baker, another Princeton star, drop-kicked a 43-yard field goal in that game for Princeton's only score.

Page 97: **Mr. Schwab or Judge Gary** Both men were captains of the steel industry. Schwab was president of Carnegie Steel and later of U.S. Steel; Gary was a former judge who organized the Federal Steel Co. for the financier J. P. Morgan.

Page 97: **President Hibben . . . "normalcy"** The president of Princeton during Fitzgerald's years at the university was John Grier Hibben, an ordained Presbyterian minister. Hibben was unhappy over the picture of Princeton drawn by Fitzgerald in *This Side of Paradise*. While campaigning for the U.S. presidency in 1920, Warren G. Harding asserted that the country needed "not nostrums but normalcy." He was ridiculed in the press for using the word; Fitzgerald's friend H. L. Mencken thought him a numbskull, an opinion Fitzgerald probably shared. Fitzgerald's application of the word "normalcy" to Hibben here is a veiled slight, as are some of the other remarks about Hibben in this essay.

Page 97: **Gauss, Heermance and Alexander Smith** Christian Gauss, professor of modern languages and later dean of the college, was Fitzgerald's undergraduate mentor. Radcliffe Heermance, director of admissions and dean of freshmen, raised admission standards for the university. H. Alexander Smith was executive secretary under President Hibben; after the war he served in the U.S. Senate.

Page 97: **Dean West** Andrew Fleming West, professor of Latin and dean of the graduate school, was the man most immediately responsible for ousting Woodrow Wilson from Princeton. He was one of the founders of the American School of Classical Studies in Rome and was responsible for creating the residential graduate college at Princeton.

Page 97: **Oswald Veblen and Conklin** Veblen came to Princeton as a preceptor in 1905 and developed into a noted research mathematician; Edward Grant Conklin was a research biologist, teacher, and public speaker interested in the philosophical implications of evolution.

Page 98: **Dr. Spaeth** J. Duncan Spaeth taught British poetry in a flamboyant style and offered one of the earliest courses in American literature to be taught at a U.S. university. He was also the rowing coach for Princeton through the 1925 season.

Page 98: **"Nassau Literary Magazine"** The *Nassau Lit*, founded in 1842, is the second oldest college literary magazine in the country. Fitzgerald published much of his early poetry and prose there.

Page 98: **the original Craig Kennedy story** Craig Kennedy was the fictional detective in a series of whodunnits written by Arthur Benjamin Reeve, a member of the Princeton class of 1903. Reeve's "The Golf Dream," the first Craig Kennedy story, appeared in the *Nassau Lit* for May 1901. Reeve transferred his character to the silent film serials; the heroine in these concoctions, named Elaine, was repeatedly rescued from the clutches of the villain by Kennedy, who always wore a white coat.

Page 98: **Henry van Dyke, David Graham Phillips, Stephen French Whitman . . . Struthers Burt** These Princeton alumni all became well-known authors. Van Dyke was a critic, novelist, and clergyman; Phillips, a descendant of Light-Horse Harry Lee, was a novelist and muckraking journalist; Whitman wrote *Predestined* (1910), a novel that Fitzgerald admired; Burt, who taught English at Princeton, wrote popular stories set in high society or in the American West.

Page 98: **Eugene O'Neill** O'Neill attended Princeton in 1906–7; in 1914–15 he studied with George Pierce Baker at Harvard before going on to his first successes with the Provincetown Players.

Page 98: **James Bruce, Forrestal and John Martin, now of "Time"**

All three men edited the *Princetonian* during their undergraduate years. After serving in the war, Bruce became a banker and diplomat; Forrestal, a naval aviator during the war, eventually was named U.S. secretary of defense; Martin worked as a journalist in England before becoming the managing editor of *Time* magazine in 1929.

Page 98: **The "Tiger"** This campus humor magazine was founded at Princeton in 1882. Fitzgerald published poems and gags in the *Tiger* during his undergraduate years. The *Lampoon, Record,* and *Widow* are the humor magazines of Harvard, Yale, and Cornell.

Page 98: **John Biggs** John Biggs, Jr., Fitzgerald's friend and roommate at Princeton, edited the *Tiger* during Fitzgerald's last year at the university. Biggs pursued a career in law and published two novels with Scribner's. After Fitzgerald's death he served as one of the executors of the author's literary estate. Biggs is mentioned in "My Generation," later in this collection.

Page 98: **Donald Clive Stuart, Mask and Wig Club** Stuart, a professor of dramatic literature at Princeton, directed Triangle Club performances from 1919 to 1934 and drew his casts entirely from the student body. The Mask and Wig Club at the University of Pennsylvania, by contrast, used professional coaches during the 1920s and sometimes recruited cast members from among the Penn alumni.

Page 98: **Roy Durstine, Walker Ellis, Ken Clark, or Erdman Harris** Roy S. Durstine, Princeton class of 1908, was president of the Triangle Club and managing editor of the *Tiger.* Walker Ellis, class of 1915, was president of Triangle during Fitzgerald's freshman year and collaborated with him on the script for *Fie! Fie! Fi-Fi!* Kenneth S. Clark, class of 1905, was editor of the *Tiger* and the *Bric-a-Brac* (the Princeton yearbook); he also worked on Triangle productions. Clark is remembered at Princeton for having written the school song "Going Back to Nassau Hall." Erdman Harris, Princeton class of 1920, wrote some of the music for *Safety First!* (Fitzgerald wrote the lyrics). Harris produced lyrics for the 1917 and 1918 Triangle productions and, in 1918, helped prevent the club from being shut down by President Hibben, who objected to drunkenness on the 1917 Christmas trip and to the risqué song lyrics and jazz melodies in the shows.

Page 99: **Prospect Street** The eating clubs at Princeton are located on Prospect Street; freshmen were forbidden to go there during

Fitzgerald's time at the university. Sophomores received bids to the clubs during Bicker Week each March.

Page 99: **Owen Johnson, in "Collier's"** Fitzgerald is remembering the photos printed in Johnson's article "The Social Usurpation of Our Colleges," in the June 15, 1912, issue of *Collier's Magazine*. Johnson wrote *Stover at Yale* (1912), a famous boys' novel which Fitzgerald read as a teenager.

Page 99: **Ivy, Cottage, Tiger Inn, and Cap and Gown** These are the four oldest of the Princeton eating clubs. Fitzgerald was a member of Cottage, which he described in *This Side of Paradise* as "an impressive mélange of brilliant adventurers and well-dressed philanderers." Greek-letter fraternities were banned at Princeton in 1855; eating clubs arose to take their place. The clubs were powerful social and political organizations on campus, and there was much jockeying for bids to the most prestigious ones.

Page 101: **Nassau Inn Bar . . . Philadelphian Society** The bar of the Nassau Inn was frequented by bibulous undergraduates in Fitzgerald's time; the Philadelphian Society was a campus religious organization.

Page 101: **"Buchmanism"** This international evangelical movement was named for its founder, Frank Buchman, who preached "world-changing through life-changing." He carried his message across the Atlantic to Oxford University in 1921, where he founded the Oxford Group.

Page 102: **David Bruce . . . Richard Cleveland . . . Henry Hyacinth Strater** Princeton undergraduates who led a movement to boycott the eating clubs in 1917. See "Princeton's Anti-Club Fight Stirs the University," *New York Times Magazine*, January 21, 1917. All three men are mentioned in "My Generation," later in this collection.

Page 102: **Edward Carpenter** This English author and clergyman renounced religion in 1874 and became a Fabian socialist. His writings on social reform include *England's Ideal* (1887) and *Civilization: Its Cause and Cure* (1889).

Page 102: **John Peale Bishop** Bishop was Fitzgerald's most avowedly literary friend at Princeton. As the editor of the *Nassau Lit*, he published some of Fitzgerald's apprentice poetry and fiction. He served as the model for Thomas Parke D'Invilliers in *This Side of Paradise* and later had success as a poet and journalist. He is mentioned in "My Generation."

Page 102: **Jack Newlin** Fitzgerald's classmate John V. Newlin, who worked with him on the *Nassau Lit*, died on August 5, 1917, of wounds suffered at Montzéville. He was awarded the Croix de Guerre posthumously.

Page 103: **Professor Wardlaw Miles** Louis Wardlaw Miles, a preceptor in English during Fitzgerald's final months at Princeton, taught courses in Anglo-Saxon and was a specialist in the works of King Ælfred.

Page 103: **Williams College** Founded in 1793, this small, exclusive college in Williamstown, Massachusetts, was still a purely undergraduate institution in the 1910s and 1920s. Princeton was developing its research and graduate programs during this period.

Page 103: **Lois Moran** Fitzgerald met this young actress in Hollywood in early 1927. He was struck by her beauty and admired her work ethic; she is the model for Rosemary Hoyt in *Tender Is the Night*. She played roles in American movies through the early 1930s and appeared on Broadway in the 1931 production of George and Ira Gershwin's *Of Thee I Sing*.

Page 103: **no Elizabethan Club as at Yale** The Elizabethan Club at Yale was founded in 1911 when an alumnus named Alexander Smith Cochran donated a major collection of Elizabethan literature, in original editions, to the university. Cochran purchased and donated a building to house the collection; the Elizabethan Club met there for discussions of literature and art.

Page 103: **wears his P on the inside of his sweater** Varsity athletes at Princeton (and elsewhere) received heavy cloth letters, sometimes called monograms, in the school colors. These were sewn onto jackets and sweaters. Wearing one's P on the inside of one's sweater was seen as a mark of modesty.

Page 103: **Attorney General Palmers or Judge Thayers . . . Secretary Mellon** Alexander M. Palmer, the U.S. attorney general in the years 1919–21, was famous for prosecuting citizens and deporting aliens during the "Red Scares." Amos Madden Thayer, a federal judge, decided an 1897 case that allowed the common law of conspiracy to be used against members of a labor union. Andrew W. Mellon, secretary of the Treasury from 1921 to 1932, was seen as a crony of big business.

"A SHORT AUTOBIOGRAPHY
(with acknowledgements to Nathan)"

Page 105: The acknowledgment in the title is to the drama critic George Jean Nathan, coeditor of *The Smart Set* with H. L. Mencken. Not all of the bar and country-club names in this piece are identifiable, nor are the drinking companions.

Page 105: **Bustanoby's** The Café des Beaux Arts at Sixth and 40th was called "Bustanoby's" after its proprietor, Louis Bustanoby. Fitzgerald caroused there as an undergraduate. He calls the establishment "Bistolary's" in *This Side of Paradise*.

Page 105: **White Sulphur Springs, Montana** In the summer of 1915 Fitzgerald vacationed at a ranch in Montana (near the city of White Sulphur Springs) owned by the family of his school friend Charles "Sap" Donahoe. He got drunk with the cowhands and won fifty dollars in a poker game. The experience gave him material for his story "The Diamond as Big as the Ritz" (1922).

Page 105: **White Bear Yacht Club** This club was located on White Bear Lake, near Fitzgerald's native St. Paul. He attended dances at the club as a teenager and lived there with his wife, Zelda, during the summer of 1922.

Page 106: **Monsignor X at the Lafayette** Monsignor Sigourney Fay, Fitzgerald's mentor at the Newman School, was the model for Monsignor Darcy in *This Side of Paradise*. The Hotel Lafayette, on 9th Street, was known for its French cuisine.

Page 106: **the Seelbach Hotel in Louisville** A fashionable hotel in Louisville, mentioned in Chapter IV of *The Great Gatsby*. For his wedding to Daisy, Tom Buchanan came to Louisville "with a hundred people in four private cars and hired a whole floor of the Seelbach Hotel."

Page 106: **Sazerac Cocktails** Concoctions of absinthe, sugar, bitters, water, and whiskey.

Page 106: **the Royalton** Fitzgerald means the Royalton Hotel, a chic caravansary on West 44th Street near Fifth Avenue.

Page 106: **the Savoy Grill** This restaurant, in the Savoy Hotel on the Strand, was favored by Americans visiting London; among its patrons were Ernest Hemingway and George Gershwin. After 1926 the Savoy Grill became known as the "American Bar."

Page 106: **Via Balbini in Rome** There is no Via Balbini in Rome. The

Via Balbo, near the Ministero dell'Interno, is a possibility; but it is more likely that Fitzgerald was thinking of Genoa and had in mind the Via Balbi, one part of the baroque thoroughfare that encircles the historic center of that city. "A Short Autobiography" was written in late March 1929, the same month in which the Fitzgeralds visited Genoa.

Page 107: *Minnewaska* . . . **Valescure** The Fitzgeralds sailed to Europe on the liner *Minnewaska* in May 1924. Valescure is a residential area near San Raphaël on the Côte d'Azur; the Fitzgeralds lived there in 1924 while he was writing *The Great Gatsby*.

Page 107: **the Seldes on their honeymoon** The American critic Gilbert Seldes, Fitzgerald's contemporary, was married in June 1923. (Fitzgerald misremembers the year, placing the honeymoon in 1924.) Seldes published a laudatory review of *The Great Gatsby* in the January 1926 issue of the *New Criterion*; he is mentioned again later in this collection in "My Generation."

Page 107: **La Reine Pédauque** Fitzgerald often lunched at this Paris restaurant. The name means "the queen with the webbed feet of a goose."

Page 107: **the Ritz sweatshop in Paris** The Ritz Bar, a popular gathering place for Americans in Paris, figures in Fitzgerald's story "Babylon Revisited" (1932).

Page 108: **St. Estèphe . . . Salies-de-Béarn** St. Estèphe is a French Bordeaux, full and robust, requiring many years to reach maturity. Fitzgerald's bottle might have needed further aging. The spa town of Salies-de-Béarn in the Pyrenees is known for its unusually salty thermal pools. Zelda took a cure there in January–February 1926.

Page 108: **La Garoupe . . . Gerald M.'s grenadine cocktail** La Garoupe is an esplanade along the shoreline of Cap d'Antibes, the resort area where the Fitzgeralds met Gerald and Sara Murphy, the American expatriates on whom Dick and Nicole Diver in *Tender Is the Night* are partly based.

Page 108: **the Ambassador bungalows** The Ambassador was a Los Angeles hotel; its bungalows were arranged around a central garden. Fitzgerald and Zelda lived there in January and February 1927 while he worked on "Lipstick," a flapper comedy he was writing for Constance Talmadge. Among their neighbors were the screen stars Carmel Myers and John Barrymore.

"GIRLS BELIEVE IN GIRLS"

Page 109: **the Castles** Vernon and Irene Castle (he British, she American) were a famous dance team of the prewar era. They began performing together in Paris in 1911 and brought their act to New York the following year. The Castles invented the Castle Walk, a version of the fox-trot with a skip-step on the upbeat.

Page 109: **Beatrix Esmond . . . Beatrice Normandy** Beatrix, the daughter of Francis Edmond in Thackeray's novel *Henry Esmond* (1852), is a beautiful, selfish coquette who attaches herself to wealthy men. Beatrice Normandy is the snobbish young aristocrat in H. G. Wells' *Tono-Bungay* (1909); she romances but later abandons the protagonist of the novel, George Ponderevo, a member of the servant class.

Page 110: **the ladies of Michael Arlen** Arlen is remembered for his short-story collection *These Charming People* (1923) and his novel *The Green Hat* (1924). Arlen's heroines are direct, honest, and sexually adventurous. Iris March in *The Green Hat* was based on the wealthy American expatriate Nancy Cunard and on Duff Twysden—who also served as a model for Brett Ashley in Hemingway's *The Sun Also Rises* (1926).

Page 111: **Elsie Janis or Ethel Barrymore** Elsie Janis, a stage and movie actress, entertained American troops in France during the war. After the war she starred in a patriotic stage production called *Elsie Janis and Her Gang* (1919). Ethel Barrymore was a popular stage actress who usually portrayed warm, wholesome characters. She is the source of the quotation that ends "Who's Who—and Why," the first essay in this collection.

Page 112: **Edna Millay, Helen Wills, Geraldine Farrar, and the Queen of Roumania** Celebrated beauties. The poet Edna St. Vincent Millay won the Pulitzer Prize in 1923 for *The Ballad of the Harp-Weaver*. Helen Wills, a tennis champion, was known for her plucky approach to the game. The American soprano Geraldine Farrar starred at the Metropolitan Opera from 1906 to 1922, often appearing in *Madame Butterfly* and *Carmen*. Queen Marie of Roumania (a granddaughter of Queen Victoria) helped to bring Roumania into the First World War on the Allied side. Her image was featured in ads for Pond's cold cream.

Page 112: **Aimee Semple McPherson . . . Ruth Snyder** Known as

Sister Aimee, this flamboyant evangelist founded the International Church of the Foursquare Gospel in 1923 and conducted services in the Angelus Temple, Los Angeles. She wore a flowing white gown and blue cape and once rode a motorcycle through the sanctuary to illustrate her sermon "The Jazz Age Is Speeding to Hell." Ruth Snyder is glossed in the notes for "Princeton."

Page 112: **Clara Bow** Known to her fans as "The 'It' Girl," Clara Bow was one of the most appealing movie actresses of the 1920s. She was famous for her sex appeal and often portrayed emancipated flappers. Her best-remembered movies are *The Plastic Age* (1925), *It* (1927), and *Dangerous Curves* (1929).

Page 115: **Praxiteles** This Athenian sculptor of the fourth century BC was famous for his *Hermes with the Infant Dionysus*, recovered in the Heraeum, Olympia, in 1877, and for *Aphrodite of Cnidus*, a copy of which is in the Vatican.

Page 115: **Gibson Girl** Pen-and-ink drawings of the Gibson Girl (named after the creator, the artist Charles Dana Gibson) appeared in *Life* magazine, on wall posters, in albums, and on pillows and scarves. The Gibson Girl had upswept hair, a long neck, and aristocratic features; she wore evening clothes or a sporting costume, usually for golf or tennis.

"THE DEATH OF MY FATHER"

Page 118: **Book of Etiquette** Emily Post was an authority on social behavior whose book *Etiquette in Society, in Business, in Politics, and at Home* (1922) went through numerous editions. She was known for using common sense to calm the social insecurities of the American bourgeoisie.

Page 119: **We walked downtown in Buffalo** The Fitzgerald family lived in Buffalo, New York, for much of Fitzgerald's boyhood—from April 1898 until January 1901 and again from September 1903 until July 1908. His father, Edward Fitzgerald, worked as a salesman for Procter & Gamble during those years.

Page 120: **Early's march** Jubal Early was a Confederate general under both Jackson and Lee during the American Civil War. He commanded troops in most of the major battles in the eastern theater of the war. In June 1863 he led his men from the Shenandoah Valley into Pennsylvania and captured the towns of Gettysburg and York—the march to which Fitzgerald refers here.

"ONE HUNDRED FALSE STARTS"

Page 122: **Ouled Nail dancers from Africa** The Fitzgeralds attended a performance by these belly-dancing prostitutes during a trip to Algeria in February 1930.

Page 122: **Grand Guignol** The name of a small theatre in Paris (and by extension of the shows given there) in which actors staged gruesome and macabre spectacles: bloody dismemberments, beheadings, and tortures—the performances leavened with a bit of Gallic sex farce. The Grand Guignol was a popular tourist attraction.

Page 122: **H. G. Wells's "History of the World"** Fitzgerald has in mind Wells' *A Short History of the World* (1922), a condensation of his *Outline of History* (1920). Fitzgerald read much fiction by Wells during his Princeton years, including *The New Machiavelli* (1911), *Joan and Peter* (1918), and *The Undying Fire* (1919).

Page 123: **"Two Little Savages" . . . "The Mysterious Island"** *Two Little Savages*, a popular 1903 juvenile book by Ernest Thompson Seton, is subtitled: *Being the Adventures of Two Boys Who Lived as Indians and What They Learned*. A translation into English of the science-fiction castaway classic *The Mysterious Island*, by Jules Verne, was first published in the U.S. by Scribner's in 1875.

Page 126: **Mr. Terhune** Albert Payson Terhune was best known for his sentimental stories about collies. His work sometimes appeared in the same issues of the *Saturday Evening Post* as Fitzgerald's. His most popular book was *Lad, a Dog* (1919).

Page 127: **Ed Wynn** This popular comedian appeared in vaudeville, theatre, movies, and radio. His goofy, yodeling voice was familiar to audiences in the 1920s; much of his humor was based on costumes and sight gags.

Page 129: **a girl named Elsie** "Elsie" is Ginevra King, Fitzgerald's first serious love, a child of wealth from Lake Forest, Illinois. She and Fitzgerald met in St. Paul in January 1915 and carried on an intense romance, largely epistolary, that flourished for six months and lasted for two years. Ginevra served as a model for

several of Fitzgerald's best-known characters, including Isabel
Borgé in *This Side of Paradise*, Judy Jones in "Winter Dreams,"
and Daisy Buchanan in *The Great Gatsby*.

Page 130: **"Business Is Good"** This two-sided paperweight survives
in the Fitzgerald collection at Princeton. The other side reads
"Keep Smiling."

Page 131: **Joseph Conrad** Fitzgerald is quoting, approximately, from
Conrad's preface to *The Nigger of the "Narcissus"*—first serial-
ized in 1897, with the preface first appearing in 1914. Conrad's
full sentence reads, "My task which I am trying to achieve is, by
the power of the written word, to make you hear, to make you
feel—it is, before all, to make you *see!*"

"AUTHOR'S HOUSE"

Page 133: **Joan Crawford, Virginia Bruce and Claudette Col-
bert** All three women were popular screen stars of the 1930s.
In the spring of 1938 Fitzgerald was put to work at Metro-
Goldwyn-Mayer to write an original screenplay for Crawford;
when he told her of the assignment, she said, "Write hard, Mr.
Fitzgerald. Write hard." Virginia Bruce appeared in more than
fifty films, including *Jane Eyre* (1934) and *The Great Ziegfeld*
(1936). Claudette Colbert excelled in comic roles; she won an
Oscar in 1934 for *It Happened One Night*, playing opposite
Clark Gable.

Page 136: **at Foyots and the Castello dei Cesari and the Escargot** Foyots, located opposite the Luxembourg Palace, was a
favorite meeting place for Americans in Paris. The Castello dei
Cesari, on the Monte Aventino in Rome, was near the graves of
Keats and Shelley in the Cimitero Protestante. L'Escargot, on
rue Montorgueil, is one of the oldest restaurants in Paris, frequented in Fitzgerald's time by Jean Cocteau, Pablo Picasso,
and Charlie Chaplin.

Page 136: **Château d'Yquems . . . Dago Red . . . Alabama white
mule** Fitzgerald is mixing the high and the low. Château
d'Yquem is an exceptionally rare amber-colored sauterne prized
by collectors; Dago Red is common Italian red wine; Alabama
white mule is clear moonshine distilled from corn mash.

Page 137: **Thomas Kracklin** A fictitious name. A female reader did
write to Fitzgerald's character Basil Duke Lee in care of the *Sat-*

urday Evening Post, asking whether he might be her half brother. Fitzgerald answered her letter, leading her on for a short while. The Basil stories were published in the *Post* in 1928–29.

Page 139: **from the Golden Gate to Bou Saada** Fitzgerald means from west to east—from the Golden Gate Bridge in San Francisco to Bou Saada, a town in Algeria that he and Zelda visited in February 1930.

"AFTERNOON OF AN AUTHOR"

Page 141: **Sam Goldwyn . . . Spessivtzewa** In March 1936, around the time he was writing "Afternoon of an Author," Fitzgerald was trying to arrange a meeting with the movie producer Samuel Goldwyn. L. G. Braun, manager of the ballerina Olga Spessivtzewa, was trying to broker a movie contract for her with Goldwyn. Fitzgerald thought he might interest all parties in an idea he had for a ballet script, but nothing came of the scheme.

Page 142: **the college campus across the way** Fitzgerald was living in Baltimore near the campus of Johns Hopkins University.

Page 144: **Stonewall Jackson's last words** According to Jackson's physician, his last words were, "Let us cross over the river, and rest under the shade of the trees." Hemingway took the title of his 1950 novel *Across the River and into the Trees* from the sentence.

Page 144: **Lee shrivelling . . . Grant with his desperate memoir-writing** Robert E. Lee withdrew from public life after the Civil War and assumed the presidency of Washington College in Lexington, Virginia (now Washington and Lee University). Unlike most of the major commanders of the war, he declined to write his memoirs. Ulysses S. Grant served as U.S. president from 1869 to 1877. In 1884 he lost heavily from investments in a fraudulent banking business and, dying of cancer, finished writing his *Personal Memoirs* only a few days before his death.

Page 144: *Venite Adoremus* The Christmas hymn known as "O Come, All Ye Faithful"—in Latin, "*Adeste Fideles.*"

Page 144: **"Maryland, My Maryland"** This is the Maryland state song (though not officially declared so until 1939, after the first publication of this essay). The song is sung to the tune of "O, Tannenbaum."

Page 145: **Turner sunset or Guido Reni's dawn** Fitzgerald means the

English Romantic painter J. M. W. Turner, known for rendering light (especially sunsets) with great evocativeness. *Aurora*, a ceiling painting in the baroque classical style by the Bolognese artist Guido Reni, is in the Palazzo Rospigliosi.

Page 146: **a story about a barber** The story is "A Change of Class," which Fitzgerald published in the September 26, 1931, issue of the *Saturday Evening Post*. Fitzgerald wrote the story in Switzerland in July 1931 and sold it to the *Post* for $4,000.

Page 147: **Lafayette statue** An equestrian statue of the Marquis de Lafayette sits on Mt. Vernon Place in Baltimore, just in front of a large monument to George Washington.

Page 147: **Man Mountain Dean** Frank Simmons Leavitt, who used the stage name "Man Mountain Dean," was a professional wrestler who played strongman roles in the movies. Fitzgerald might have seen him with Jean Harlow and William Powell in *Reckless* (1935) and with Joe E. Brown in *The Gladiator* (1938).

"AN AUTHOR'S MOTHER"

Page 149: **Alice and Phoebe Cary** The sisters Alice and Phoebe Cary collaborated on sentimental poems and stories. *The Poetical Works of Alice and Phoebe Cary* was a backlist staple for Houghton Mifflin during the 1870s and 1880s. The poem "about the girl instructing the artist" is "An Order for a Picture."

Page 150: **Mrs. Humphry Ward . . . Edna Ferber** Ward, a granddaughter of Thomas Arnold, wrote popular novels about philanthropy and religion. Ferber was best known for her novel *Show Boat* (1926), which became a successful musical on Broadway.

"MY GENERATION"

Page 154: **Buster Brown collars** The comic strip *Buster Brown*, drawn by R. F. Outcault, featured Buster, an ideal American boy, and his talking bulldog Tige. Buster's clothing became popular for small boys; he wore a sailor cap, large white collar, bow tie, belted jacket, and knickers.

Page 154: **the Fleet was being sent on a trip** In 1907–9, President Theodore Roosevelt sent the U.S. Atlantic Fleet on a trip around the world to demonstrate American naval power. The convoy consisted of sixteen new battleships and a "Torpedo Flotilla" of six early destroyers. Because the battleships were painted white, the ships were referred to collectively by the press as the "Great White Fleet."

Page 154: **Cervera's fleet** At the beginning of the Spanish-American War, Pascual Cervera y Topete, admiral of the Spanish fleet in the Atlantic, took his ships into the harbor of Santiago de Cuba, where he was blockaded by American ships from May until July 1898. He ordered his captains to run the blockade; the Spanish ships were destroyed; Cervera was captured.

Page 155: **"finally only the names of places had dignity . . ."** From Chapter XXVII of *A Farewell to Arms*. The passage begins, "There were many words that you could not stand to hear and finally only the names of places had dignity."

Page 156: **General Winfield Scott . . . at Bull Run** Scott was a hero of the War of 1812 and the Mexican War. He argued early in the Civil War that battle should be delayed until a civilian army had been trained and equipped properly. His counsel was ignored, resulting in disaster for the Union at the first battle of Bull Run, July 21, 1861.

Page 156: **One of us recently married Hedy Lamarr!** The Austrian film star Hedy Lamarr, known for her femme fatale roles, married the forty-three-year-old film producer Gene Markey in Mexicali on March 4, 1939. Fitzgerald would have seen her on the film lot; both he and she were under contract to Metro-Goldwyn-Mayer in 1938.

Page 156: **post-Fauntleroy suits** *Little Lord Fauntleroy*, a sentimental story by Frances Hodgson Burnett, inspired a style of children's clothing (black velvet suit, lace collar, flowing tie) based on the illustrations by Reginald Birch in the 1886 first edition.

Page 156: **toy boats called the *Columbia* and the *Reliance*** These U.S. yachts, skippered by the American yachtsman Charles Barr, won three America's Cup competitions during Fitzgerald's boyhood. The *Columbia* was victorious in 1899 and 1901, the *Reliance* in 1903.

Page 157: **the Russo-Japanese war** A war fought in 1904–5 between Russia and Japan over which country was to have dominance in Manchuria and Korea. The Japanese won by bottling up the Russian fleet at Port Arthur.

Page 157: **"Life"** This weekly picture magazine, founded by Henry Luce, was a pioneer publication in the field of photojournalism.

Issues of *Life* sometimes included pictures of cute American children at play—hence Fitzgerald's reference here.

Page 158: **"We're in the army now"** Fitzgerald has in mind "You're in the Army Now," authorship uncertain, a song popular during the First World War and later wars. The best-known stanza goes this way: "You're in the army now, / You're not behind a plow; / You'll never get rich, / You son-of-a-bitch, / You're in the army now!"

Page 158: **Hack McGraw** Curtis Whittlesey ("Hack") McGraw was a member of the class of 1919 at Princeton. In the First World War he fought in the Meuse-Argonne offensive and was wounded at Ivergny. After the armistice he returned to Princeton and was captain of the football team in 1919. McGraw spent his professional life at McGraw-Hill publishers, a firm founded by his father.

Page 158: **Tommy Hitchcock** An aviator with the Lafayette Escadrille during the war, Hitchcock was shot down and imprisoned by the Germans but escaped to Switzerland and eventually to Paris. After the war he became the best polo player of his generation in the U.S. He stood as a partial model for both Tom Buchanan in *The Great Gatsby* and Tommy Barban in *Tender Is the Night*. Fitzgerald met him in May 1923.

Page 158: **Society Islands** This group of French-controlled islands in the southern Pacific includes Tahiti and Bora-Bora. The Polynesian inhabitants were encouraged to wear Western dress by Christian missionaries—hence Fitzgerald's comment about "shirts on girls."

Page 158: **Ernest Hemingway . . . the massacres in Smyrna** Greek forces occupied the Turkish seaport of Smyrna in 1919. The Turks recaptured the city in September 1922 and killed many of the Greek occupiers. Hemingway reported on these events for *The Toronto Daily Star*. Some of the interchapters in his short-story collection *In Our Time* (1925) are drawn from this experience, as is "On the Quai at Smyrna," first published in the Scribner's 1930 second American edition of the book.

Page 158: **Ben Hecht and Charlie MacArthur** Both men began as newspaper writers in Chicago. Later they collaborated on plays and film scripts, including *The Front Page* (1928) and *Twentieth Century* (1934). Fitzgerald and MacArthur were friends and drinking companions on the French Riviera in the summer of 1926.

Page 158: **Dempsey . . . Tunney** Jack Dempsey, a popular heavy-weight, won the world title from Jess Willard in 1919 and held it until 1926, when he lost to Gene Tunney in a ten-round decision in Philadelphia. Tunney, who regarded boxing as a science, defeated Dempsey again in a rematch in 1927. This second fight included an infamous "long count." Tunney was knocked down by Dempsey in the seventh round and benefited from extra time to recover, owing to the referee's mistake.

Page 158: **Donald Peattie** This prolific nature writer published a book called *Flowering Earth* in 1939, around the time Fitzgerald was writing "My Generation."

Page 158: **George Antheil's music** Antheil, an American composer of ultra-modern music, is remembered for *Le ballet méchanique*, scored for player pianos, automobile horns, electric bells, and an airplane propeller. The work was performed in Paris in 1926 and in New York in 1927—both times to hostile reactions. In 1936 Antheil moved to Hollywood, where he wrote music for feature films.

Page 158: **Paul Nelson's suspended house** Nelson left Princeton in 1917 to join the U.S. Air Force. He fought in the Meuse offensive and at Argonne, and after the war he became a celebrated architect. Fitzgerald is thinking of Nelson's "Maison Suspendue" of 1936–38, a structure composed of prefabricated units suspended in a steel cage.

Page 158: **Vincent Youmans . . . "Oh Me, Oh My, Oh You"** This American songwriter wrote the scores for the musical *No, No, Nanette* (1925) and for the first Fred Astaire–Ginger Rogers movie *Flying Down to Rio* (1933). Among his standard songs are "Tea for Two" (1925), "More Than You Know" (1929), and (with the lyricist Ira Gershwin) "Oh Me, Oh My, Oh You" (1921).

Page 159: **Merian Cooper . . . to make "Chang" and "Grass"** Cooper was the first Hollywood producer fully to embrace Technicolor. He was celebrated during the 1920s for *Grass* (1925), about the Bakhtiari tribe of Persia, and *Chang* (1927), a popular elephant movie. He is remembered today for producing the classic film *King Kong* (1933).

Page 159: **Denny Holden** Holden, whom Fitzgerald had known as a student at Princeton, became a flying ace with the French Air Service during the First World War and later flew for the French during the Moroccan uprising of 1924. He died in November 1938 in a plane crash near Sparta, Tennessee.

Page 159: **Tom Wolfe left the Norfolk ship-yards** As a teenager, the writer Thomas Wolfe worked in the shipyards at Newport News, Virginia, and wrote about the experience in *Look Homeward, Angel*, his first novel—edited by Maxwell Perkins and published by Scribner's in 1929.

Page 159: **Mumford** Lewis Mumford was a historian, architectural critic, and urban planner who analyzed the effects of urbanization and technology on human societies. Fitzgerald probably knew his books *Sticks and Stones* (1924) and *The Brown Decades* (1931). Edmund Wilson and Gilbert Seldes are glossed above, pp. 171 and 180.

Page 159: **Sherwood and Behrman, Barry and Stallings** American dramatists of Fitzgerald's generation. Robert Sherwood, a pacifist and antifascist, won Pulitzer Prizes for *Idiot's Delight* (1936) and *Abe Lincoln in Illinois* (1938). S. N. Behrman wrote witty comedies of manners, including *The Second Man* (1927) and *Rain from Heaven* (1934)—the latter among the first American plays to recognize the Nazi threat. Philip Barry specialized in sophisticated drama about the wealthy; his best-known play is *The Philadelphia Story* (1939). Laurence Stallings collaborated with Maxwell Anderson on *What Price Glory?* (1924)—one of the first realistic American dramas about the war.

Page 160: **Frank Capra and King Vidor** Capra and Vidor were prominent Hollywood film directors who enjoyed near-total artistic control over their movies. Capra made optimistic, sentimental comedies at Columbia Pictures, including *It Happened One Night* (1934). Vidor is remembered for *The Big Parade* (1925), *Our Daily Bread* (1934), and *The Citadel* (1938).

Page 160: **Bill Tilden . . . Dudley Mudge . . . Harrison Johnston** "Big Bill" Tilden, a colorful tennis player who dominated the game for more than a decade, won at Wimbledon in 1920 and was a frequent competitor in Davis Cup matches. Harrison R. ("Jimmy") Johnston, a top U.S. amateur golfer during the 1920s, helped the U.S. to win the Walker Cup in 1924, 1928, and 1930. Dudley Mudge, a lesser-known golfer, was a medallist in the U.S. Amateur tournament in 1915.

Page 160: **Herbert Agar and novelists Cyril Hume and Edward Hope (Coffey)** Agar, an American journalist and historian, won the 1933 Pulitzer Prize in History for *The People's Choice: From Washington to Harding*. Hume was the author of several novels, including *Wife of the Centaur* (1923). Coffey, a member of the

Princeton class of 1920, supplied the lyrics for the three Trian-
gle shows immediately after Fitzgerald had left the university.
Under the name "Edward Hope," he wrote the novel *She Loves
Me Not* (1934), which was turned into a Broadway comedy
and a successful Hollywood movie (starring Bing Crosby and
Miriam Hopkins).

Page 160: **Elliott Springs . . . Hamilton Fish Armstrong** Elliott
White Springs wrote *War Birds: Diary of an Unknown Aviator*
(1926), an account of aerial combat in the First World War.
Fitzgerald might have seen the unproduced screenplay for
War Birds to which MGM held production rights in the early
1930s; William Faulkner worked on the script in November
and December 1932. Armstrong was an influential diplomat,
editor, and writer. He edited the quarterly *Foreign Affairs* for
fifty years; Fitzgerald probably knew his books *Hitler's Reich*
(1933) and *Can America Stay Neutral?* (1939). John Biggs is
identified on p. 176.

Page 161: **Spence Pumpelly and Charlie Taft did the same at
Yale** Fitzgerald is thinking of a period at Yale, from approxi-
mately 1913 to 1917, during which the secret society system
was subjected to heavy criticism from a group of undergradu-
ates. Among the leaders of this group were Spencer Armstrong
Pumpelly, who later pitched for the Washington Senators, and
Charles Phelps Taft, a son of former U.S. President William
Howard Taft (himself a member of the Yale law faculty by then).

Page 161: **when any moppet . . .** A reference by Fitzgerald to his
daughter, Scottie, who had published a piece entitled "A Short
Retort" in the July 1939 issue of *Mademoiselle*. Scottie does not
mention her father in the text of her article, but it is by-lined
"by Frances Scott Fitzgerald, daughter of F. Scott Fitzgerald,
whose novels of the Jazz Age are definitive records of an era."
Scottie wrote in part, "In the speakeasy era that followed, we
were left pretty much to ourselves and allowed to do as we
pleased. And so, we 'know the score.'" Fitzgerald probably
wrote "My Generation" as a response to Scottie. He was not
pleased by her remarks: he wrote to his agent, Harold Ober, "I
didn't like the idea of her sitting on my shoulder and beating my
head with a wooden spoon" (July 8, 1939).

Page 161: **"The Jungle" and "The Octopus" . . . John Steinbeck ate
the grape of wrath** References to novels that exposed various
ills in American society: Upton Sinclair's *The Jungle* (1906),

Frank Norris' *The Octopus* (1901), and John Steinbeck's *The Grapes of Wrath* (1939).

Page 161: **manifest destiny** Supporters of Manifest Destiny argued for the continued territorial expansion of the United States. The term was used frequently during the annexation of the American Southwest and Northwest and, later, during the occupation of various islands in the Pacific.

Page 161: **to paraphrase Sir Edward Grey** At dusk on August 3, 1914, Edward, Viscount Grey of Fallodon, was watching the lamplighters in London's St. James's Park from the windows of his room in the Foreign Office. He said, "The lamps are going out all over Europe; we shall not see them lit again in our lifetime."

Page 161: **Dr. Hutchins, Peter Arno . . . Irving Thalberg, Caldwell and O'Hara, Saroyan and Odets . . . Lindbergh and . . . Dewey were all too young** While president of the University of Chicago, Robert Maynard Hutchins devised the influential "Chicago Plan," which involved the establishment of a four-year liberal arts college divorced from the university's professional schools. Peter Arno published satirical cartoons of clubmen and dowagers in the *New Yorker*. Irving Thalberg, a talented Hollywood producer of the 1930s, was the model for Monroe Stahr in Fitzgerald's *The Last Tycoon* (1941). Erskine Caldwell was famous for *Tobacco Road* (1932) and *God's Little Acre* (1933). The novelist John O'Hara, who became friendly with Fitzgerald during his last period in Hollywood, was the author of *Appointment in Samarra* (1934) and *Butterfield 8* (1935). William Saroyan and Clifford Odets were successful playwrights of the 1930s. Charles Lindbergh made the first solo nonstop transatlantic flight in May 1927. Thomas Dewey became governor of New York in the 1940s and was the Republican nominee for U.S. president in 1944 and 1948.

Page 162: **the Grizzly Bear and the Bunny Hug** Scandalous dances invented in San Francisco waterfront dives during the early 1900s. Fannie Brice introduced the Grizzly Bear to New York audiences in the *Ziegfeld Follies* of 1910; Mae West was arrested for performing the dance in 1913. The Bunny Hug involved grinding, shaking, and wiggling to slow blues tunes.

Page 162: **"Beautiful Katy"** Fitzgerald is thinking of "K-K-K-Katy," a popular "tongue-tied" song by Geoffrey O'Hara. The music publisher Leo Feist called it the "Sensational Stammering Song Success Sung by the Soldiers and Sailors."

Page 162: **Picasso says** Fitzgerald is taking Picasso's statement from a passage in Gertrude Stein's *The Autobiography of Alice B. Toklas* (1933), a book he admired. Stein writes, "As Pablo once remarked, when you make a thing, it is so complicated making it that it is bound to be ugly, but those that do it after you they don't have to worry about making it and they can make it pretty, and so everybody can like it when the others make it." Picasso was speaking of Robert Delaunay and his followers and of the Futurists—artists who he felt had copied his work and vulgarized his ideas.

Page 162: **a line of Willa Cather's** From the last sentence of Cather's *My Ántonia* (1918): "Whatever we had missed, we possessed together the precious, the incommunicable past."

Acknowledgments

For assistance in the preparation of this collection the editor thanks Eleanor Lanahan, Thomas P. Roche, Jr., and Chris Byrne, Trustees of the F. Scott Fitzgerald Estate; Phyllis Westberg of Harold Ober Associates, Inc.; Don Skemer, Curator of Manuscripts at Princeton University Library; Linda Bree, Literature Publisher at Cambridge University Press; Peter Nelson, a close reader of Fitzgerald's texts; and Jeanne Alexander and Michael DuBose at Penn State.

About the Author

F. Scott Fitzgerald was one of the major American writers of the twentieth century—a figure whose life and works embodied powerful myths about our national dreams and aspirations. Fitzgerald was talented and perceptive, gifted with a lyrical style and a pitch-perfect ear for language. He lived his life as a romantic, equally capable of great dedication to his craft and reckless squandering of his artistic capital. He left us one sure masterpiece, *The Great Gatsby*; a near-masterpiece, *Tender Is the Night*; and a group of stories and essays that together capture the essence of the American experience. His writings are insightful and stylistically brilliant; today he is admired both as a social chronicler and as a gifted artist.

Fitzgerald was born in St. Paul, Minnesota, on September 24, 1896. His father, Edward Fitzgerald, was descended from Maryland gentility; he was well-bred and mannerly but lacked commercial acumen and, after a series of business failures, was forced to rely on his wife's family for support. Fitzgerald's mother, Mollie McQuillan, was an intelligent, eccentric woman whose Irish immigrant father had made a success in St. Paul as a wholesale grocer. The Fitzgeralds lived conventionally—"In a house below the average / On a street above the average," wrote young Fitzgerald in a poem. As a boy he was precocious: handsome and socially observant, he wrote plays for the local dramatic society and produced fiction and poetry for the school newspaper. In 1911 his parents sent him east to a Catholic prep school, the Newman School in Hackensack, New Jersey, where he came under the influence of a sophisticated priest, Monsignor Sigourney Fay, and an Anglo-Irish author named Shane Leslie. These two men ignited his literary ambitions and encouraged him to develop his talents as a writer.

Fitzgerald entered Princeton in the fall of 1913. He was captured immediately by the beauty of the university and by its aura of high striving and achievement. He labored under social disadvantages there—he was a Midwesterner and an Irish Catholic—but his enthusiasm and literary talent won him some successes. He wrote lyrics for the musical comedies produced by the Triangle Club, published fiction and poetry in the *Nassau Literary Magazine*, and accepted a bid to the prestigious Cottage Club. He was an indifferent student, however, and his poor marks eventually caught up with him, denying him the campus awards he had desired. Fitzgerald never took a degree from Princeton; he made a semi-honorable exit from the university in 1917, answering the call to colors and serving as an army officer in the First World War.

To his great regret, Fitzgerald "didn't get over." His battalion was waiting in New York to embark for Europe when the armistice was signed in November 1918. Fitzgerald never saw the front, but the war years were momentous for him in other ways. In the summer of 1918, while in training camp near Montgomery, Alabama, he met Zelda Sayre, a beautiful and unconventional southern belle, the daughter of a prominent local judge. Fitzgerald fell in love with her—with her passionate nature and adventurous spirit—and they became engaged. After his discharge from the army he took a job in an advertising agency in New York City, determined to make a success in business. But Fitzgerald was a failure as an ad man; he hated the work and chafed at his separation from Zelda. She lost faith in him, believing that he could not support her, and broke off their engagement in June 1919. After an epic bender, Fitzgerald quit his advertising job and spent his last few dollars on a train ticket home to St. Paul. He meant to prove himself to Zelda by writing a novel. "I was in love with a whirlwind," he later recalled, "and I must spin a net big enough to catch it out of my head."

Fitzgerald began this improbable quest by resurrecting the typescript of a novel that he had been calling *The Romantic Egotist*. He had finished the narrative during army training camp, working on it in the officers' club during nights and weekends. The book had been rejected twice by Charles Scribner's Sons, a prestigious New York publishing house, but a young editor there named Maxwell Perkins had recognized Fitzgerald's talent and had told him to keep trying. During the summer of 1919, working diligently in the attic of his parents' home in St. Paul, Fitzgerald reconceived *The Romantic Egotist* and transformed it into *This Side of Paradise*, a daring and experimental novel that mixed prose, poetry, and drama dialogue. Perkins accepted the book in September for publication the following spring.

Backed by this success, Fitzgerald rekindled his romance with Zelda. They renewed their engagement and were married in St. Patrick's Cathedral in New York on April 3, 1920, just a week after publication of *This Side of Paradise*. The novel was an immediate hit, with enthusiastic reviews and excellent sales. Fitzgerald became famous overnight. He found that he was in great demand as a writer: his price for stories rose quickly, and he began to produce much commercial short fiction—a dependable source of money for the extravagant life that he and Zelda now were leading. These triumphs in literature, love, and finances gave Fitzgerald great faith in his star. "The compensation of a very early success is a conviction that life is a romantic matter," he later wrote. "In the best sense one stays young."

For Fitzgerald the early 1920s were productive. He published a second novel, *The Beautiful and Damned*, in 1922; it marked an advance over *This Side of Paradise* in form and style, though it lacked the energy and charm of the earlier book. Fitzgerald also wrote some of his best short stories during these years—prophetic tales like "May Day" and "The Diamond as Big as the Ritz" and perceptive character studies like "Dalyrimple Goes Wrong" and "The Ice Palace." He and Zelda lived near New York, in a cottage in Westchester County; later they rented a house on Great Neck, Long Island, where they socialized with the Manhattan literati and the Broadway theatre crowd.

In the spring of 1924 the Fitzgeralds and their young daughter Scottie, born in 1921, traveled to Europe and settled on the French Riviera. Fitzgerald needed quiet and freedom from distraction in order to compose his third novel. He labored through the summer and by October had completed a narrative called "Trimalchio"—a short, well-crafted novel of manners set on Long Island. His hero was a hazily depicted parvenu from the Midwest named Jay Gatsby. Fitzgerald mailed the novel to Perkins in New York, and Perkins had it set in type for spring publication. Fitzgerald continued to work on the text in galley proofs, however, rewriting two chapters, sharpening Jay Gatsby's character, and infusing the story with an aura of myth and wonder. The novel, now titled *The Great Gatsby*, was published in April 1925. Reviews were good but sales disappointing. In the years that followed, however, *Gatsby* would win much praise and ascend to a high place in the American literary canon. Today it is one of the most widely read American novels of the twentieth century.

The Great Gatsby established Fitzgerald as a skilled professional. This is one of the paradoxes of his life: though he was sometimes frivolous and irresponsible in his personal behavior, he was thoroughly serious as an artist. He had a good understanding of the marketplace and was ambitious and self-critical, aiming to create a body of writing that would survive him. His struggles to balance work against amusement, popular appeal against literary artistry, energized his career and gave complexity to the fiction he wrote.

The Fitzgeralds remained in Europe during the late 1920s. These were years of growth for Fitzgerald; he read and traveled and observed, "seeking the eternal Carnival by the Sea" and capturing in his fiction the exoticism of the great European cities. He knew James Joyce, Gertrude Stein, Sylvia Beach, Sinclair Lewis, and Archibald MacLeish; his closest friends were Gerald and Sara Murphy, a sophisticated American couple who later served as partial models for Dick and Nicole Diver in *Tender Is the Night*. Fitzgerald also met a talented young writer named Ernest Hemingway and became friends with him for a time. Their relationship, however, was eventually eroded by competition and jealousy, mostly on Hemingway's part.

The Fitzgeralds' marriage began to disintegrate during their last few years in Europe. Fitzgerald's drinking increased as he struggled to produce a new novel; he managed to write some excellent short fiction, including the Basil Duke Lee stories of 1928 and 1929, but failed to make much progress on the manuscript of his book. Zelda's health deteriorated as she worked fervently to construct a life of her own as a ballet dancer. Talented and restless, she wanted an identity apart from her role as Fitzgerald's wife. The strain of ballet training helped to bring about a mental breakdown in 1930 from which she never entirely recovered.

The small family returned to America in 1931. Fitzgerald managed to complete his novel, *Tender Is the Night*, while living in Baltimore. Scribner's published the book in April 1934 to generally good reviews but, again, to only moderate sales. Fitzgerald was greatly disappointed; he had worked on the book for nine years, putting the manuscript through some seventeen drafts. *Tender Is the Night* shows evidence of this labor on every page; it is a brilliantly written study of expatriate life, but its flashback structure causes difficulty for readers, and the fall of its hero, Dick Diver, seems overly precipitate.

Fitzgerald's personal life went into decline after the novel was published. His health, never strong, had been damaged by the push to finish the book, and his personal troubles had left him creatively and financially drained. Zelda was being treated at Johns Hopkins Hospital and later in clinics near Asheville, North Carolina. In good periods she and Fitzgerald lived together, but the reconciliations were never successful or lasting. Zelda had begun to paint and write, producing an autobiographical novel called *Save Me the Waltz*. She and Fitzgerald had quarreled bitterly about her use of autobiographical material in the novel. Scribner's had published the book in 1932, but not before Zelda, at Fitzgerald's insistence, had reworked the narrative. Scottie, the Fitzgerald's daughter, had flourished during the years in Europe, but now her parents could not provide her with a stable home. She spent her teenage years in eastern boarding schools and during most vacations stayed with the family of Harold Ober, Fitzgerald's literary agent.

Fitzgerald reached a professional crisis in the mid-1930s. He found that he could no longer manufacture the light, entertaining tales of love that he had sold for many years to *Redbook, Metropolitan*, and the *Saturday Evening Post*. While living in North Carolina he began to write for *Esquire,* a new magazine, and published three autobiographical "Crack-Up" essays there, famous today as dissections of the American Dream and as measured reflections on failure and loss. At the age of forty he found himself emotionally bankrupt, "standing at twilight on a deserted range, with an empty rifle in my hands and the targets down."

Fitzgerald was rescued in the summer of 1937 by Harold Ober, who arranged a lucrative Hollywood contract for him. He went to the West Coast in July and worked as a screenwriter for Metro-Goldwyn-Mayer for eighteen months, paying off his debts to Scribner's and Ober. He established a relationship with the newspaper columnist Sheilah Graham, who took care of him and endured his erratic behavior. Fitzgerald began his stint in Hollywood with high hopes but quickly became disillusioned. He was temperamentally unsuited for movie work and resented the requirements of the studio system, which dictated that he collaborate with other scriptwriters. Despite his frustrations Fitzgerald was a diligent breadwinner, sending Scottie to Vassar College, where she wrote plays and was a popular student. Zelda lived intermittently with her family in Montgomery; her health was fragile, and she spent periods of instability, by her own choice, in the Highland Hospital in Asheville.

MGM declined to renew Fitzgerald's contract at the end of 1938, and he returned to magazine writing. In October 1939 he began a novel about Hollywood; the hero, called Monroe Stahr, was based on the movie producer Irving Thalberg. Fitzgerald was excited about the project and made good headway on his manuscript, but his health began to fail in 1940 and in late November of that year he suffered a mild heart attack. After a brief convalescence he resumed work on his novel; he died unexpectedly of a second attack on December 21. The drafts of the novel were published as *The Last Tycoon* in 1941. This incomplete novel shows great promise and provides a tantalizing glimpse of Fitzgerald's spare, mature style. He was buried in Rockville, Maryland, a town not far from his father's birthplace. Zelda lived on until March 1948, when she perished in a fire at the Highland Hospital. She was buried beside her husband in Rockville.

In his working notes for *The Last Tycoon*, Fitzgerald wrote, "There are no second acts in American lives," but his own life has been resurrected and reexamined by two generations of biographers and historians. His victories and defeats mirror the triumphs and downfalls of American society during the boom years of the twenties and the bust years that followed. His writings embody lessons of ambition and disappointment, idealism and disenchantment, success and failure and redemption, all of which are central to the American experience. During his short professional career he won a wide audience and helped to establish American authors as deserving of serious attention. His romantic readiness for life and his gift for hope have come to embody important aspects of the American identity. He was among the first to recognize his country's dreams of infinite possibility. Fitzgerald's works and life still fascinate us, and his reputation continues to grow.

J.L.W.W. III